NEW DIRECTIONS FOR ADULT AND CONTINUING EDUCATION

Ralph G. Brockett, *University of Tennessee, Knoxville*
EDITOR-IN-CHIEF

Alan B. Knox, *University of Wisconsin, Madison*
CONSULTING EDITOR

Rethinking Leadership in Adult and Continuing Education

Paul J. Edelson
State University of New York, Stony Brook

EDITOR

Number 56, Winter 1992

JOSSEY-BASS PUBLISHERS
San Francisco

RETHINKING LEADERSHIP IN ADULT AND CONTINUING EDUCATION
Paul J. Edelson (ed.)
New Directions for Adult and Continuing Education, no. 56
Ralph G. Brockett, Editor-in-Chief
Alan B. Knox, Consulting Editor

Microfilm copies of issues and articles are available in 16mm and 35mm,
as well as microfiche in 105mm, through University Microfilms Inc., 300
North Zeeb Road, Ann Arbor, Michigan 48106.

LC 85-644750   ISSN 0195-2242   ISBN 1-55542-729-4

NEW DIRECTIONS FOR ADULT AND CONTINUING EDUCATION is part of The
Jossey-Bass Higher and Adult Education Series and is published quarterly
by Jossey-Bass Inc., Publishers, 350 Sansome Street, San Francisco,
California 94104-1310 (publication number USPS 493-930). Second-class
postage paid at San Francisco, California, and at additional mailing offices.
POSTMASTER: Send address changes to New Directions for Adult and
Continuing Education, Jossey-Bass Inc., Publishers, 350 Sansome Street,
San Francisco, California 94104-1310.

SUBSCRIPTIONS for 1992 cost $45.00 for individuals and $60.00 for institutions, agencies, and libraries.

EDITORIAL CORRESPONDENCE should be sent to the Editor-in-Chief, Ralph
G. Brockett, Dept. of Technological and Adult Education, University of
Tennessee, 402 Claxton Addition, Knoxville, Tennessee 37996-3400.

Cover photograph by Wernher Krutein/PHOTOVAULT © 1990.

The paper used in this journal is acid-free and meets the strictest
guidelines in the United States for recycled paper (50 percent
recycled waste, including 10 percent postconsumer waste). Manu-
factured in the United States of America.

10% POST
CONSUMER
WASTE

CONTENTS

EDITOR'S NOTES

Adult and continuing education is a field of action and intense involvement. As in other "frontline" educational settings, the task of keeping up with the pace of the work is a test of imagination and at times endurance. Work within administrative environments can also involve a struggle with an endless range of obstacles and constraints, if not frustrations. The impetus and pressures to act on immediate problems are often so great that there is insufficient time for reflective analysis on important issues that appear to fall outside of day-to-day concerns.

For example, we often take for granted the organizational goals and workplace structures that circumscribe our behavior. Since in many cases these predate our affiliation with our institutions, there is a tendency to assume that these conditions have a life of their own, independently of human volition. Yet lately, concerns with productivity and efficiency throughout modern societies have created a more critical environment for questioning the status quo. Professionals within adult and continuing education programs, units, and divisions are being challenged to step back and reconsider their missions and how these can be achieved within leaner fiscal environments. Leadership, that special quality that helps galvanize human action, has become a much sought after trait in this current context of change, uncertainty, and decreasing confidence in both the value and continuity of routinized practice.

With these challenges in mind, the purpose of this volume, *Rethinking Leadership in Adult and Continuing Education*, is to help readers reflect on leadership in education, an important but enigmatic topic. In thinking and writing about leadership, we also want to know what makes some people effective leaders, in part to find the secret ingredients or skills and develop them in ourselves. It is a natural impulse to desire improvement in our activities; and as people professionally involved in adult and continuing education, we place confidence in our abilities to study leadership and improve our mastery of its craft.

A major thesis of this book is that a shift in our thinking about leadership has already taken place. The old leadership paradigm was based on a view of the adult and continuing education function as a production-oriented organizational subunit that generated "programs" or training "packages" and then marketed them to student "consumers." From this viewpoint, generally known as the machine-production model, leadership activities were heavily influenced by issues of production and distribution.

In contrast, the new leadership paradigm is grounded in a different organizational perspective, that of the "learning organization." Within this framework, the priorities for adult and continuing education have become more diverse and entail interaction with the host organization and outside constituencies. Here, a broader definition of adult education, incorporating the continuing education "workplace," challenges leaders to expand their activities beyond a concern for programs into new interpretations of adult education that can encompass many more knowledge-creating projects. Leadership in this context is less hierarchical and more decentralized, team oriented, and empowering. In essence, adult and continuing education practitioners model the behaviors that they desire to impart to students—as mutually supporting lifelong learners with diverse objectives.

The chapters of this volume have been developed to explore various aspects of leadership in adult and continuing education and also to stimulate a climate of critical inquiry about other issues affecting the field. Thus, the first three chapters emphasize the analysis of context from both organizational and individual perspectives. In Chapter One, I set the stage by questioning traditional organizational models that influence our understanding of adult and continuing education as a prelude to reconceptualizing the leader's role in matters pertaining to programs, policies, politics, people, and the profession. In a similar vein, in Chapter Two, Joe F. Donaldson examines how leaders are usually socialized into their positions and describes new ways of gaining fresh perspectives on their roles by teaching. In Chapter Three, Laurent A. Parks Daloz and I look at how the social context of work can be viewed through the lens of staff development. We recommend mentorship as a way of rethinking the meaning of collegial relationships within adult and continuing education programs.

The next three chapters demonstrate how adult and continuing education leaders can influence the development of their organizations by defining and expanding their roles. In Chapter Four, Judith L. McGaughey uses the concept of symbolic leadership to draw attention to how adult and continuing education leaders can help their institutions respond to the new pluralism. In Chapter Five, Manuel London discusses leadership in the human resources development context, emphasizing the important responsibility of creating a continuous learning environment for the entire organization. And, in Chapter Six, James C. Novak shows how adult educators interested in continuing professional education can apply the concept of reflective practice to alter the roles of professionals within their organizations and within the society at large.

The final two chapters highlight different ways in which adult and continuing education leaders can prepare themselves to address the challenges of the future. In Chapter Seven, Amy D. Rose provides insight into the extensive research on leadership as a means of helping professionals develop their own research agendas. In Chapter Eight, I illustrate how leaders can orient themselves to the future of adult and continuing education so that they are in a better position to deal with uncertainty and doubt.

This final chapter also recapitulates a major theme of the volume: A prime leadership responsibility is to let go of assumptions based on routine practice, comforting but misleading conventional understandings, and views of leadership that inhibit others from leading and pointing the way.

In closing, I thank the chapter authors, series editor Ralph Brockett, and the many people with whom I have worked over the years who have collaborated in my ongoing experimentations in this least traditional of fields, adult and continuing education. A special note of gratitude is due my wife Leta and to Shari and Avi for encouraging me to persevere.

Paul J. Edelson
Editor

PAUL J. EDELSON is dean of the School of Continuing Education and director of the Continuing Education Research Center at the State University of New York, Stony Brook.

We need to move beyond traditional views of leadership that are
rooted in production-oriented models of adult and continuing
education and begin reconceptualizing work, learning, and leadership
within adult and continuing education organizations.

Rethinking Leadership in Adult and Continuing Education

Paul J. Edelson

We think of leadership as a catalytic quality that can energize an entire
organization. Whether in the task of motivating others or in areas of
specialized decision making, it is that extra ingredient that seems to make
a difference in how a program, unit, or division functions and achieves its
goals. Gardner (1986c, p. 5) addresses nine tasks that he considers most
compelling for the leader: envisioning goals, affirming values, motivating,
managing, achieving a workable level of unity, explaining, serving as a
symbol, representing the group externally, and renewing. Leadership can
also include the daunting challenge of creating an optimal working environment for members of the organization.

It might be argued that American society, with its excessive emphasis
on individualism, places a premium on leadership as a special type of
heroic behavior and thereby promotes a distorted conception of the role of
"leaders" at the expense of "followers." In light of what many now believe
is necessary for maximum participation by members of society, we should
critically examine our unstated assumptions about leadership so as to
determine whether our interpretations of this behavior contribute to the
evolution of our society in directions of greater mutual participation and
democracy. In fact, Gardner's (1986a, p. 23) concept of "transforming
leadership" turns this dilemma upside down by challenging leaders to
transform their followers into leaders! A similar point is made by Kanter
(1984), who articulates a vision of "empowerment" that has had a far-
reaching impact on how we view the contemporary workplace.

Certainly, our response to leadership in adult and continuing education is culture-bound and therefore heavily influenced by the traditions

NEW DIRECTIONS FOR ADULT AND CONTINUING EDUCATION, no. 56, Winter 1992   © Jossey-Bass Publishers

passed on to us from other institutions in our society, especially the military, the church, and the corporation. The first two in particular, because of their historical persistence over thousands of years, have become organizational archetypes and serve as models for how we frame our thinking about organizations today. Sometimes, without being aware, we erect our own intellectual scaffolding on these foundations. Concepts of leadership stressing hierarchy and prophetic wisdom from above can be traced to examples furnished by religious traditions, both Eastern and Western. The imagery of omniscient generals ordering thousand of troops into battle furnishes still another, albeit principally male, metaphor of command. Recently, the corporate world has been the source of much of the contemporary leadership literature—both popular (Iacocca, 1984) and scholarly (Porter, 1985)—and has furnished concepts that are applied to the nonprofit sector, including education.

The identification of leadership with hierarchy has been challenged by those studying informal organizational culture who have found that leadership is widely dispersed within the organization (Deal and Kennedy, 1982; Kanter, 1984). Yet, some positions are always thought of as leadership positions, and it is axiomatic that the higher an individual rises in an organization the greater the expectation for the person to exercise leadership in connection with increased authority, notwithstanding Gardner's (1986b, p. 6) observation that those in high positions and status do not necessarily lead. All executives, including directors of continuing education, simply cannot avoid the expectations of both superordinates and subordinates to provide leadership.

Customarily, leadership behavior, as Gardner suggests (1986c, p. 5), shapes organizational goals and provides guidance and motivation for others in achieving those objectives. But the persistent, highly reductionistic view whereby the leader, through some special insight, attempts to predict or chart the future and then take other people there makes leadership a scarce commodity, concentrated in well-defined roles, including director, dean, department chair, principal, president, or superintendent. Is this view of leadership still valid?

In today's highly specialized workplace, leaders cannot know how the most important jobs within their organizations are or will be performed in terms of content, resource requirements, and future directions. These details of job description and performance are increasingly established by professionalized incumbents who are responding to their own sets of opportunities and constraints established by the evolution of knowledge in their fields. In fact, the information flow may be reversed when these professionals tell the organization's "leader" what they need or where the organization should be headed. Moreover, Cohen and March (1986) question the ability of leaders to function in a complex, nonlinear environment when the coupling of cause and effect is frequently attenuated and blurred. Birnbaum (1988) and Senge (1990) call for "cybernetically" attuned leaders who can see the patterns and relationships underlying seemingly random or disconnected events.

Are we then drawn to the conclusion that more leadership in the conventional military or corporate mode of dynamic and forceful action can be less of a good thing? Mintzberg's (1973) characterization of the administrative work environment as brief, varied, and fragmented resonates with many adult and continuing education practitioners. With the leader's attention drawn in many different directions, leadership can be a fiction. Too busy to take the time to lead and drowning in administrivia, the leader cannot focus on any one thing long enough to grasp its details. Under these circumstances, the compulsion to lead, in the sense of decisiveness amidst uncertainty, can promote action for action's sake and thereby undo or undermine even sound plans.

Clearly, or perhaps not so clearly, as we look at how we view organizations and how they should function, principles and activities of leadership are being actively questioned. Thus, the stage is set for our rethinking of leadership within adult and continuing education.

Contexts of Adult and Continuing Education

The developing literature in adult and continuing education is drawing greater attention to contextual dimensions of practice (Jarvis, 1985; Merriam and Caffarella, 1991; Usher and Bryant, 1990; Collins, 1991). Usher and Bryant (1990), in particular, stress the notion of "situatedness" as an organizing concept. This includes not only the administrative context of the adult and continuing education unit, or even the host or parent organization, but also how the institution of adult and continuing education as a whole is located or situated within society. Context also includes the functions that the institution does or does not fulfill, as well as the constituencies who are served and those who are excluded.

Drawing on an earlier body of literature by Freire (1970), to which we could also add Bowles and Gintis (1976), Giroux (1983), and Shor (1986), Usher and Bryant (1990) draw attention to the reproduction function of formal education institutions in our society. In their use of the term reproduction function, all of these authors are referring to how education recapitulates the fundamental structures and values of society. In the case of North America, these structures and values define a middle-class perspective that both suppresses and marginalizes the perspectives of minorities, the working class, people of color, and women. The value of situatedness as an analytical tool is that it helps us to step back from our routines and look at the larger context within which we operate, enabling us to realize that our own lives in institutions as both workers and leaders shape our worldview and perpetuate a bias that is difficult to escape.

Once we realize and accept that our actions are never unbiased or value free, we can begin to understand the many factors underlying our decision making. Thus, effective leadership behavior entails clarification and confrontation of our hidden biases in addition to resolution of the immediate issues we encounter as officeholders performing our jobs. For example, decisions about curriculum expansion in adult and continuing education could be framed in conventional organizational terms of how to expand markets already served by a hypothetical organization (postbaccalaureate degree holders) or in terms of populations that are not addressed by the school's adult education programs (unemployed adults). Simply by discussing the issue of who is or is not being served, we can generate a great deal of new thinking about underlying educational and social values and perhaps galvanize new programs.

This approach to thinking about our behavior is closely related to Schön's (1983) concept of reflection-in-practice, in particular, double-loop learning in which practitioners reflect on the act of reflecting and consider alternate ways of framing reality. Part of the task of rethinking leadership requires us to break out of conventional institutional frames of reference that guide our thinking and behavior.

But to continue our investigation of leadership in adult and continuing education, we must first start with the immediate organizational context. Adult educators work within a broad range of organizations and perform multiple roles (Darkenwald and Merriam, 1982; Merriam and Cunningham, 1989). Public schools, colleges and universities, business and industry, government agencies, and nonprofit organizations constitute some of the more obvious and popular settings. The place of adult and continuing education within these settings is variable in that in some cases adult education may be the primary raison d'être or goal of the organization, driving other organizational objectives. An example is a nonprofit organization exclusively devoted to training physically challenged adults. Adult education leadership within these circumstances is coterminous with the major direction or purpose of the organization. In many cases, however, adult education as a mission or set of goals exists as a secondary or tertiary function, competing with other organizational goals or priorities.

The actual roles or positions held by adult educators within organizations are within the two broad employment categories of administration or instruction, which means that staff either primarily administer or teach. Research can be a third independent axis, but it typically should be viewed as reflective and analytical activity that is a part of the other two dimensions.

Meanings of Adult and Continuing Education Leadership

Although the duties of adult and continuing education leaders vary with the size of the adult education program or unit and the nature of the parent organization, there is enough consistency throughout the profession to categorize leadership of and for adult and continuing education as follows: program leadership, policy leadership, political leadership, leadership of people, leadership within the profession.

Program Leadership. Among the five categories of leadership considered here, program leadership may well be the first among equals. The program, that is, the deliverables of adult and continuing education, is the central point of existence of the whole enterprise (Knowles, 1980; Sork and Caffarella, 1989; Offerman, 1987). It is how the organization speaks to constituencies. But the program is more than a structural framework, delivery system, or form of packaging. It is also what most people, particularly students and other significant audiences, perceive as the reality or essence of adult and continuing education. Successful program management is thus key to the education unit's viability. It is safe to say that without programs there can be no adult and continuing education.

Beyond fulfilling some measure of the organization's education goals, programs are a means of generating resources for the institution. These may take the form of student credit hours, tuition revenue, community goodwill, and production of a trained work force, to cite some of the more powerful motivators. Even altruistic goals such as improving the local economy, helping people obtain better jobs, and generating creative options for the use of leisure time can be looked at from a systems perspective that links attainment of these worthwhile objectives to the ongoing existence of the sponsoring organization. Program leadership requires an understanding of the nuances of these exchange relationships and the factors that influence program development.

At its fundamental level, a program review or analysis becomes a form of marketing audit (Kotler, 1982) whereby the adult and continuing education director obtains a detailed understanding of all of the factors associated with the unit's programs. Concepts such as competitive strategy (Baden, 1987), flanking and extension strategy (Pappas, 1987), and portfolio review (Matkin, 1988) as well as an understanding of the essential importance of program quality (Freedman, 1987) all come into play.

Heavy reliance on a production-line model of program development has given birth to the "program shop" in adult and continuing education practice wherein industrial machine metaphors and scientific management concepts borrowed from the corporate sector, especially techniques of assembly-line mass production, are not out of place. This highly tuition- or enrollment-driven model can be found in both the private and public sectors and poses a genuine risk for adult and continuing education even when it appears successful. For example, the tendency for high-enrollment courses or programs to drive out those with low enrollments, a type of Gresham's law in adult and continuing education, can distort an institution's extension program. If programmers chase markets instead of causes, adult and continuing education will surely become the property of those with the ability to pay. To illustrate this market-driven dimension of adult and continuing education, I use the metaphor of a sailboat pushed along by a combination of wind and current (Edelson, 1991a).

Our challenge is to think of leadership beyond issues of enrollment, sections, revenue, and full-time equivalents and to look more deeply into aspects of adult and continuing education professionalism to identify other dimensions of leadership. For example, Galbraith (1991) offers insight into alternative education environments for programs. Freedman (1987) challenges practitioners to identify quality and mission as a prelude to program development. Wlodkowski (1985) examines teaching and learning in the adult education classroom and how instructors can use motivational techniques to improve their effectiveness. And Collins (1991) identifies leadership with vision and understanding of adult education, not with proficiency in technocratic processes. Real leadership in program development will rely increasingly on a broader knowledge base in adult and continuing education in addition to the already substantial knowledge base on marketing and administrative organization.

Policy Leadership. Adult and continuing education programs do not exist by themselves in a vacuum. They are inextricably linked to larger organizational and contextual issues, including policy. Continuing education policy, that is, what the organization believes it should be doing in the area of adult education, derives from the parent organization's broader goals and values, as expressed not only in official mission statements but also in the day-to-day realities of organizational practices and procedures.

Policy can be viewed as a type of consensus or agreement, whether a snapshot fixed in time in the form of a written document or a temporary resting point based on recent deliberations. Giroux (1983) cautions against a neutral or conflict-free interpretation of consensus that eliminates from consideration contesting and alternative viewpoints. He maintains that by accepting consensus as a neutral given, we compromise options for future change based on alternative scenarios.

Adult and continuing education leaders should take existing policy as a point of departure for developing their own policies and action plans. Existing statements and assumptions that guide adult education policy must be reexamined and deconstructed to determine their meanings and to see if they are still valid guides. Many institutional statements on the goals of adult and continuing education were written long ago and have become a type of boilerplate or encrustation that can girdle and suffocate an institution. A self-study conducted with an advisory committee of staff and other organizational colleagues can often galvanize new thoughts and actions on adult education and is a valuable task for leadership.

We should be mindful that the development of mission statements has become a necessary ritual in modern organizations. Senge (1990) cautions against the temptation of leaders to impose, top down, their own definitions of mission and vision on other members of the organization. He maintains that truly energizing mission statements tap significantly into the desires and aspirations of those numerous others who work side-by-side with the leader. These mission statements, which recognize and incorporate the views of colleagues, produce a synergistic whole that is greater than the sum of its parts and the key to superperforming organizations.

Political Leadership. Adult and continuing education leaders, as heads of subsystems within larger organizations, are always functioning politically in that they are motivated by a set of unique goals or interests arising from the mission and activities of their units, which are in competition, or even conflict, with those of other subunits. The foci or points of contention involve more than budgetary resources, although fiscal issues can always be a source of struggle. Units are continuously competing for influence on the goals of the organization as they are expressed in specific actions or issues that emerge in routine activities. Scheduling decisions, hiring policies, curriculum—all of these can precipitate political activity by individuals on behalf of larger groups.

To provide a context for understanding the political arena of adult and continuing education directors, I have previously characterized the role of the dean or director of continuing education as a diplomat charged with the responsibility of representing this emerging "state" within a university federation made up of other schools and divisions (Edelson, 1990). Leadership behavior is thus focused on the political goals of developing a sense of identity or nationhood for continuing education that includes independence and autonomy in all of its relationships and emphasizes the need for alliances and treaties as ways of securing objectives.

In considering the political leadership exercised by an adult and continuing education director, it is necessary to remember that though the leader's power and authority are granted by superordinates, he or she leads on behalf of subordinates. The leader's dual loyalties to superordinates and subordinates contribute to role conflict, as the leader is pulled between competing and contradictory demands (Katz and Kahn, 1966). The implementation of directives from "above" that are not popular with staff is a typical political situation encountered in the real-life world of administration. Often, at the heart of the problem are different perceptions of the place and value of adult and continuing education within the organization. Suffice it to say that simple rules of thumb about what to do in these circumstances are suspect. Effective political leadership tends to favor compromise, a pragmatic approach to problems, and a search for acceptable or "satisficing" solutions (Birnbaum, 1988, p. 58) that are not always perfect. As a consequence, some idealistic people avoid thinking about and cultivating the political dimensions of their roles. Yet, political leadership is a fact of life that must be acknowledged by adult and continuing education directors, if only to protect their units from harm.

Leadership of People. Ironically, our current conceptions of organizations as complex, nonlinear, open systems (Birnbaum, 1988; Cohen and March, 1986) deemphasize the historical role of the leader as a type of superhero with larger-than-life physical and metaphysical qualities. We have come to appreciate the dependence of leaders on "followers," and now even that term has been redefined in a more egalitarian way as "colleagues" (Bennis and Nanus, 1985, pp. 119–129). I do not believe that this linguistic shift is merely a cloaking device for the hierarchical redeployment of power. Rather, it represents an acceptance of the importance of an organization's human capital, especially in its intellectual dimensions, to the generation of value—those worthy goals that the organization seeks to accomplish.

Tendencies to decentralize leadership, coupled with the increased use of specialized work teams for specific management projects, multiply the opportunities for many more people within the organization to develop and improve their leadership skills. Scanning, thinking, and planning for the future should be team projects, where the leader's role is to get things started and then step aside, allowing the group to "run itself" (Heider, 1986, p. 33).

Leadership in these circumstances requires the preparation of colleagues to accept greater responsibility for autonomy in directing their own work in nonroutinized ways. Once agreement has been reached on objectives, people must be free to structure and develop their own approaches. For this decentralized management style to be effective, there is a need for periodic feedback, which can be in the form of meetings, reports, and, perhaps most important, informal conversations in order to recalibrate efforts and directions if necessary.

Daloz's (1986) observation that we must care for students as people as much as we care for what they accomplish in class extends to the leadership venue as well. A view of staff as just workers is too limiting. A mutual perspective as colleagues learning about adult and continuing education from each other, as "friends helping each other" (Collins, 1991, p. xii), can enlarge the constrained and pressured world of work and make it more significant and rewarding. People who view explorations into adult education as connected to their own developmental quests will naturally forge stronger bonds of attachment and approach their practice in more analytical and inspired ways.

Leadership Within the Profession. The field of adult and continuing education transcends separate institutions and incorporates diverse realms of practice. It is in fact a constellation of myriad worlds and orientations. Brockett (1989) provides an overview of professional organizations in adult education that can be characterized as different interpretations of adult and continuing education.

Shelton and Spikes (1991) discuss the benefits of participation in professional organizations, including the development of leadership skills. Collins (1991) more critically views professional associations as gatekeepers, controlling and restricting professional dialogue within a field. He directly addresses the historical role of associations in restricting entry to fields and maintaining monopolies of skills and bodies of knowledge on behalf of existing professional groups.

Yet, granting the validity of some of Collins's observations, we cannot deny that associations serve the important function of focusing attention on problems, challenges, and issues within adult and continuing education and are thus a vehicle for progress. For this reason, leaders who wish to make an imprint or to influence the evolution of adult and continuing education must accept the responsibility of participating in professional organizations, aside from the professional development benefits that may accrue to them.

An Ambivalence Toward Leadership and a Challenge

Despite the opportunities within adult and continuing education, there is evidence that some deans and directors, even when successful, are unwilling to remain in the field (Edelson, 1991b). In two of the cases that I studied, the incumbents, who were successfully meeting institutional expectations for adult and continuing education, nevertheless saw their positions as temporary way stations or stepping-stones en route to other administrative roles. Baden (1991), in analyzing the career development of adult and continuing education leaders, constructed three models of career success. In the first model, incumbents make a long-term commitment to the field. In the second model, they move laterally within the college out of continuing education and into other administrative areas. In the third model, they more broadly apply their vision of education within the college to other student constituencies.

Does the much discussed marginality of adult and continuing education promote this outward mobility, or are we simply noting a natural desire of incumbents to search out new professional experiences and areas of personal challenge? More research in this area is needed before we can draw any conclusion that the adult education field is less hospitable to purposeful career development. The preliminary findings do, however, point out the constant need for new leadership. Therefore, it is an inescapable observation that one of the essential leadership responsibilities in adult and continuing education is to prepare a greater number of people to lead. A strong egalitarian tradition in adult education reinforces this call.

Adult and continuing education leaders are aware that there has never been a situation of "business as usual" in the field. Changing institutional needs, uncertain funding patterns, declining or burgeoning regional economies, new organizational players, and the larger political milieu all contribute to an environmental flux. The concepts of transformative leadership and empowerment mentioned earlier reflect a recognition of the uncontainable centrifugal forces driving our organizations. We need to constantly assess the ways in which we lead so that the field of adult education continues to fulfill its mandate of providing opportunity and choice in the decades ahead.

References

Baden, C. (ed.). *Competitive Strategies for Continuing Education.* New Directions for Adult and Continuing Education, no. 35. San Francisco: Jossey-Bass, 1987.

Baden, C. "Continuing Higher Education: Reflections on Leadership and Success." *Journal of Continuing Higher Education,* 1991, *39* (1), 23–25.

Bennis, W. G., and Nanus, B. *Leaders: The Strategies for Taking Charge.* New York: HarperCollins, 1985.

Birnbaum, R. *How Colleges Work: The Cybernetics of Academic Organization and Leadership.* San Francisco: Jossey-Bass, 1988.

Bowles, S., and Gintis, H. *Schooling in Capitalist America.* New York: Basic Books, 1976.

Brockett, R. A. "Professional Associations for Adult and Continuing Education." In S. B. Merriam and P. M. Cunningham (eds.), *Handbook of Adult and Continuing Education.* San Francisco: Jossey-Bass, 1989.

Cohen, M. D., and March, J. G. *Leadership and Ambiguity.* (2nd ed.) Boston: Harvard Business School, 1986.

Collins, M. *Adult Education as Vocation.* New York: Routledge & Kegan Paul, 1991.

Daloz, L. A. *Effective Teaching and Mentoring: Realizing the Transformational Power of Adult Learning Experiences.* San Francisco: Jossey-Bass, 1986.

Darkenwald, G. C., and Merriam, S. B. *Adult Education: Foundations of Practice.* New York: HarperCollins, 1982.

Deal, T. E., and Kennedy, A. A. *Corporate Cultures: The Rites and Rituals of Corporate Life.* Reading, Mass.: Addison-Wesley, 1982.

Edelson, P. J. "The Dean of Continuing Education: A Diplomatic Model." *Journal of Continuing Higher Education,* 1990, *38* (2), 29–33.

Edelson, P. J. "Model Building and Strategic Planning in Continuing Higher Education." *New Horizons in Adult Education,* 1991a, *5* (2), 15–25.

Edelson, P. J. "Transitions: Research on the Success of Newer Deans and Directors of Continuing Education." Paper presented at the annual meeting of the National University Continuing Education Association, Miami, Florida, April 20–23, 1991b. (ED 336 542).

Freedman, L. *Quality in Continuing Education: Principles, Practices, and Standards for Colleges and Universities.* San Francisco: Jossey-Bass, 1987.

Freire, P. *Pedagogy of the Oppressed.* New York: Seabury, 1970.

Galbraith, M. W. (ed.). *Adult Learning Methods.* (2nd ed.) Malabar, Fla.: Krieger, 1991.

Gardner, J. W. *Leadership and Power.* Leadership Paper No. 4. Washington, D.C.: Independent Sector, 1986a.

Gardner, J. W. *The Nature of Leadership: Introductory Considerations.* Leadership Paper No. 1. Washington, D.C.: Independent Sector, 1986b.

Gardner, J. W. *The Tasks of Leadership.* Leadership Paper No. 2. Washington, D.C.: Independent Sector, 1986c.

Giroux, H. A. *Theory and Resistance in Education.* South Hadley, Mass.: Bergin & Garvey, 1983.

Heider, J. *The Tao of Leadership: Leadership Strategies for a New Age.* New York: Bantam Books, 1986.

Iacocca, L. *Iacocca: An Autobiography.* New York: Bantam Books, 1984.

Jarvis, P. *The Sociology of Adult and Continuing Education.* New York: Routledge & Kegan Paul, 1985.

Kanter, R. M. *The Change Masters.* New York: Simon & Schuster, 1984.

Katz, D., and Kahn, R. L. *The Social Psychology of Organizations.* New York: Wiley, 1966.

Knowles, M. S. *The Modern Practice of Adult Education: From Pedagogy to Andragogy.* (Rev. ed.) New York: Cambridge Books, 1980.

Kotler, P. *Marketing for Nonprofit Organizations.* Englewood Cliffs, N.J.: Prentice Hall, 1982.

Matkin, G. W. "Portfolio Management in Program Planning." *Continuing Higher Education Review,* 1988, 52 (3), 123–132.

Merriam, S. B., and Caffarella, R. S. *Learning in Adulthood: A Comprehensive Guide.* San Francisco: Jossey-Bass, 1991.

Merriam, S. B., and Cunningham, P. M. (eds.). *Handbook of Adult and Continuing Education.* San Francisco: Jossey-Bass, 1989.

Mintzberg, H. *The Nature of Managerial Work.* New York: HarperCollins, 1973.

Offerman, M. J. "Matching Programmatic Emphases to the Parent Organization's Values." In R. G. Simerly and Associates, *Strategic Planning and Leadership in Continuing Education: Enhancing Organizational Vitality, Responsiveness, and Identity.* San Francisco: Jossey-Bass, 1987.

Pappas, J. P. "Strategic Market Planning in Conglomerate Continuing Education Programs." In C. Baden (ed.), *Competitive Strategies for Continuing Education.* New Directions for Adult and Continuing Education, no. 35. San Francisco: Jossey-Bass, 1987.

Porter, M. *Competitive Advantage.* New York: Free Press, 1985.

Schön, D. A. *The Reflective Practitioner: How Professionals Think in Action.* New York: Basic Books, 1983.

Senge, P. M. *The Fifth Discipline: The Art and Practice of the Learning Organization.* New York: Doubleday/Currency, 1990.

Shelton, E., and Spikes, W. F. "Leadership Through Professional Associations." In R. G. Brockett (ed.), *Professional Development for Educators of Adults.* New Directions for Adult and Continuing Education, no. 51. San Francisco: Jossey-Bass, 1991.

Shor, I. *Culture Wars: School and Society in the Conservative Restoration, 1969–1984.* New York: Routledge & Kegan Paul, 1986.

Sork, T. J., and Caffarella, R. S. "Planning Programs for Adults." In S. B. Merriam and P. M. Cunningham (eds.), *Handbook of Adult and Continuing Education.* San Francisco: Jossey-Bass, 1989.

Usher, R., and Bryant, I. *Adult Education as Theory, Practice, and Research: The Captive Triangle.* New York: Routledge & Kegan Paul, 1990.

Wlodkowski, R. J. *Enhancing Adult Motivation to Learn: A Guide to Improving Instruction and Increasing Learner Achievement.* San Francisco: Jossey-Bass, 1985.

PAUL J. EDELSON is dean of the School of Continuing Education and director of the Continuing Education Research Center at the State University of New York, Stony Brook.

Thinking about leadership can often become routinized and limited by understanding gained through conventional approaches to administrative roles. This chapter describes how the role of teacher provides avenues for rethinking and strengthening leadership in adult and continuing education.

Reconfiguring the Leadership Envelope: Teaching and Administration

Joe F. Donaldson

We develop our concepts of leadership in response to what we perceive as the practice of adult and continuing education administration. Thus, there is a tendency for administrators to view leadership within the envelope of conventional administrative tasks such as planning, staffing, and managing, all of which relate to central concerns for program development and for maintenance and enhancement of the adult and continuing education organization. This conventional envelope and the forms of practice that it supports tend, however, to establish barriers between adult and continuing educators and the richness of human activity and meaning that are embedded in the programs that they administer.

A major thesis of this chapter is that these barriers diminish leadership and organizational effectiveness in adult and continuing education. To be effective, administrators need ways to overcome these barriers and, in so doing, to reconfigure the leadership envelope within which they work. Although many avenues exist to accomplish this goal, teaching is one that holds much promise. Yet, it is an avenue little traveled by most continuing education administrators.

This chapter has two purposes. The first is to consider how the conventional leadership envelope was originally established in adult and continuing education and to examine how the envelope continues to create barriers to understanding. The second is to explore how teaching, both inside and outside of one's own program, can serve to break down barriers, contributing to educators' fuller understanding of the rich reality of their programs.

NEW DIRECTIONS FOR ADULT AND CONTINUING EDUCATION, no. 56, Winter 1992   © Jossey-Bass Publishers

Learning Leadership

Our understanding of leadership is colored by our prior administrative and leadership experiences, courses, readings, socialization into the adult and continuing education profession, and attitudes about leadership that are extant in the culture. For example, we draw on concepts of leadership found in the management and adult education literature to guide our practice. These tend to be management and product oriented and based on pragmatic and practical concerns (for example, Simerly and Associates, 1987; Baden, 1987). The adult education administrative literature also draws heavily on concepts and empirical evidence from management, thus failing to deal fully with the particular realities of continuing education practice or the aims and purposes to which administrative action is addressed (Courtenay, 1990). As a consequence, we are guided as much or more by generic management and leadership concepts as by those that are particular to our practice.

Another influential source of learning about leadership is the workplace. The effect that the practice context has on our understanding of leadership cannot be underestimated: It is the common ground for adult educators, since we do not share similar backgrounds or professional preparation (English, 1992). Thus, it tends to serve as a major, unifying guide to what we understand about the field and leadership within it.

The practice context also serves as an important socializing agent. This socialization is especially important for those new to the field, since it is the major source of initial information about the knowledge, values, attitudes, and behaviors that are required. For those who have been prepared in graduate programs of adult and continuing education (either in preparation for entry or while practicing), the practice context adds dimensions of reality and specificity to the socialization that they receive in their studies. The learning that is acquired through socialization involves not only individual agents of socialization but also our interactions with others.

In the case of leadership, important individual agents of socialization are those individuals who currently hold positions of leadership. In some instances, these leaders may become mentors of those who aspire to leadership positions, assisting in their learning and development. In other situations, informal learning occurs as individuals observe the behavior of leaders and model their own behavior accordingly. The resulting behavior may be in several directions—either emulating or rejecting the leadership behaviors observed, or perhaps creating a fusion of different approaches (Bandura, 1986).

Another source for learning is through our interactions with others while we are in leadership positions. In this case, we respond to our own and others' views about what behavior is expected in the leadership role (Katz and Kahn, 1978). This role-defining and role-taking behavior may commence through anticipatory socialization (Merton, 1968), as we consider the prospect of assuming a leadership role. We reflect on what we currently understand about the role, and we gather additional information about it. Expectations of what is required, albeit minimal, are also conveyed to us in formal position announcements. More detailed understanding is gained later in the search process through job interviews. However, this emotionally charged environment provides imperfect and fleeting glances of the terrain and is limited by the number of people (as well as their understanding of the job) selected to meet with the aspirant during the screening process (Edelson, 1991).

If appointed, the new incumbent attempts to reconcile preliminary impressions and understandings with role messages and other information that he or she now begins to obtain firsthand. This is the principal reality context for testing and calibrating behavior against the expectations of superiors, colleagues, and staff, all of whom have definite points of view about what the leader's actions should be. Role-taking behavior as well as socialization into the realities of the practice context constitute a continuing process of learning based on others' responses to the new leader's fine-tuning of his or her behavior and adjustments to new role messages and senders.

Learning also occurs through participation in the continual negotiation and development of the organization's cultural norms and standards. These cultural norms, in often subtle and tacit ways, guide individuals' actions as well as the collective behavior of organizational members (Schein, 1985). This type of learning draws our attention to the role that organizational culture—in particular, the subculture of adult and continuing education administration—plays in the socialization process. It also draws our attention to the need to examine the ways in which this subculture can limit our views of leadership.

Subculture of Adult and Continuing Education Administration

Although the practice arenas for leadership in adult and continuing education vary, the overall picture is of a set of educational administrators who deal year-round with management issues. With the notable exceptions of part-time adult education directors in the public school arena and training directors in business and industry, who may also have teaching responsibilities (Yule, 1979), most adult education administrators are involved on a full-time basis with their administrative responsibilities. Teaching is generally not included as a job responsibility.

This is particularly the case for administrators of continuing higher education. Although in recent studies (Hentschel, 1990; National University Continuing Education Association, 1990) over 29 percent of the respondents (54 percent of deans and directors) had prior experience in college and university teaching, teaching is not generally a required or associated duty of continuing higher education administrators, especially those in the United States. Further, neither the proficiencies (Knox, 1987) nor the roles and responsibilities (English, 1992) developed for continuing higher education administrators require them to also be teachers.

In addition, continuing education administrators apparently, in general, do not teach in their own programs. An informal poll of approximately fifty administrators attending a recent national conference session on teaching and total quality management in continuing higher education revealed, for example, that only a handful had taught within their own programs. In some cases, participants indicated that their reluctance to enter the classroom was based on their desire to avoid a potential conflict of interest that they or their superiors believed is inherent to such teaching. But the overwhelming majority had not previously considered teaching as a possible component of their jobs (Edelson, 1992).

Adult educators in business and industry present a similar picture. More empirical evidence is available about the degree to which human resources development professionals teach. But their extent of teaching (especially those in primarily administrative roles) probably differs little from that of continuing higher education administrators. For example, while some human resources development professionals do not teach as a regular part of their jobs (Shipp, 1985), others spend approximately 11 percent of their time teaching (Yule, 1979). In marked contrast to proficiencies developed for university continuing educators, however, teaching or training is frequently included in the lists of competencies developed for this particular group of educators (Watkins, 1991).

This lack of extensive involvement in teaching by adult and continuing educators results in either an exclusive or primary focus on management and leadership, around which an organizational subculture develops. This subculture is established through a variety of means: regular interaction among administrators both at and away from work; a striving for group self-consciousness and identity, especially at the national level; shared problems in performing their duties (for example, managing personnel, planning and promoting programs, and networking with external constituencies); and action on the basis of collective understanding (for example, the need to build internal support) (Van Maanen and Barley, 1984).

Although development of a subculture may be essential to administrators' work, it also can serve to separate and insulate them from the realities of the programs that they administer. As a result, administrators only get to know their programs' instructors and learners in limited, partial, and secondhand ways. Essentially, the relationship with them is one of procurement, in which exchange of value (a central concept of marketing) provides meaning for the relationship (Edelson, 1992). Needs, motivations, and aspirations of learners are understood as group norms and trends, not as manifestations of individual personalities and environments. Learners are referred to as clients, not as individuals with unique names, faces, problems, and life situations. Instructors are known on the basis of their subject matter expertise, their ability to teach adults, and the power with which they attract an audience. To the extent that administrators know only partially and in abstract ways these other important people in the programs, they also have incomplete knowledge of the programs for which they provide leadership.

Thus, the ways in which administrators learn about leadership and the organizational subculture that develops around the management and leadership functions create a leadership envelope that is characterized by a focus on conventional administrative responsibilities and tasks. This envelope is also fitted with a cultural boundary that, while supporting and maintaining its members, also creates a barrier to people and to knowing. The envelope needs to be opened if administrators are to explore ideas that differ from managerial conventions and if they are to establish direct contact with others outside the boundary so that they can learn of different experiences and perspectives and can come to know more completely what it means to teach and what it means to learn in their own programs. Teaching can open this envelope.

Teaching, Learning, and Leadership

To understand how teaching can help administrators span the boundary of the administrative subculture, various dimensions of the relationship between teaching and leadership need to be explored. This first requires us to recognize that it is the learning obtained through and from teaching, and not the act of teaching itself, that contributes most to the opening of the conventional leadership envelope.

Two major kinds of learning can occur as a consequence of teaching: personal and organizational. Although both are fostered to some extent by most teaching situations, differences in what is learned are affected by (1) the degree to which the content taught is related to the practice of continuing education, (2) whether the learners taught are adults, and (3) whether administrators teach in their own programs or in programs sponsored by another organization or by another unit of their organization (in the case of continuing higher educators, for example, teaching in the resident, on-campus program).

Personal Learning. Three kinds of personal learning can occur as a result of teaching. The first kind is theoretical learning, or the learning of principles or concepts. Through teaching, administrators are required to remain current in their chosen fields. Study of the concepts and principles of those fields, whether existing or emerging, allows them to add to their store of knowledge and to gain deeper insight into and understanding of the domains that the principles and concepts address.

The second kind of personal learning is responsive learning. By assuming the role of teacher, adult and continuing education administrators gain increased insight into the challenges that instructors face in teaching, including the challenge of balancing the various demands that teaching puts on their time in relation to their other duties, and, in the case of teaching in their own programs, insight into the special challenges, time demands, and joys that come from working with adults in a continuing education setting. An illustration of this type of learning is provided by a continuing education administrator who was teaching in his program for the first time: "I understood the 'night school' experience as an adjunct faculty member would: being at school after work when I was both hungry and tired, meeting with rushed students in classrooms that could be too cold or too hot, and furnished with uncomfortable chairs. The logistics of offering a course could be frustrating. Was there chalk, a lectern; what were the bookstore or library hours? . . . I found teaching to be a juggling act in which I could not limit the number of balls I was forced to keep in the air" (Edelson, 1992).

The literature of adult and continuing education is replete with descriptions of continuing educators on the frontlines of their organizations. Yet, the instructors of continuing education programs have more direct contact with individual adult learners than most programming unit administrators can ever hope to experience (Donaldson, 1990). Teaching in their own units has the effect, therefore, of putting continuing educators on the frontline in another way—in direct, personal contact with the adult learners whom they serve. This individual contact provides continuing educators with information about the perspectives that these adults use to evaluate their continuing education experiences and the benefits derived from them, information that continuing educators can never fully obtain from student evaluations, contact with client group representatives, or incidental contact with individual students. This form of high-quality information is acquired, for example, by getting to know students as individual learners, learning about how they perceive the continuing education operation and about their experiences with it, and gaining insights about how the quality of students' learning experiences affects their recruitment to programs and their retention in them.

This type of learning can occur, however, only if administrators critically examine these experiences and begin to truly understand their programs from the perspectives of program instructors and adult learners. Although this kind of learning can result in explicit knowledge, the experience of teaching also contributes to an implicit, tacit knowing of what it means to be an instructor and a learner, whether in one's own program or in another's.

The practice of putting themselves in another's role allows administrators to learn about the perspectives that others have about their programs and their administration of them, perspectives that more than likely differ from those that they had prior to the experience. Knowledge about these different perspectives, whether explicit or implicit, creates what Cell (1984) calls a "productive tension" with the individual's preexisting ideas. This tension leads to "transsituational learning," or learning that results in a change in the administrator's ability to interpret a situation, either through enhancement of his or her store of perspectives or through their transformation (Mezirow and Associates, 1990). Thus, this learning contributes to a type of knowing about the programs that transcends the knowledge normally required to manage them, the knowledge of the conventional leadership envelope. In addition, as administrators' interpretations of the realities and meanings become more consonant with those of instructors and learners, they become more able to assist and facilitate the instructional process. Consequently, responsive learning enables administrators to enhance their roles as educational, and not just organizational, leaders.

The third kind of personal learning is reflective learning. To the extent that what is learned in the previous two kinds of learning is related to practice, administrators have an opportunity to employ that learning to reflect *on* as well as *in* their own practice (Schön, 1987). Instructional preparation provides time, for example, that administrators rarely get to reflect on practice, to focus on their actions and those of others with whom they work so that these actions can be evaluated not only in light of what administrators already know but also in light of what is being learned through teaching. As a result, they have the opportunity to reinterpret experiences and situations, identify gaps in their own and others' performance, and to conceptualize ways for improving their own and others' practice (Lewis and Dowling, 1992).

The content of what is taught also adds to the store of images and ideas that, according to Schön (1987) and Cervero (1988), constitutes professionals' practical knowledge, knowledge that is employed on a day-to-day basis in defining the problems encountered and in making judgments about those problems. Therefore, by teaching and having to remain current in a field, continuing educators are provided with ideas that can assist them in reflecting both on and in their practice.

The tie between teaching and reflective learning is most obvious for teaching situations in which content comes from adult and continuing education or related fields. Yet, because continuing education practice can also be informed by other disciplines and professions (Apps, 1985), other content can also be used to inform reflection. The learning that can be derived from the perspectives of other fields is another example of transsituational learning. Contrasting views are again employed to provide a multiplicity of perspectives on the same phenomena. When taken together, however, these multiple points-of-view provide a more thorough understanding of a situation than an individual could achieve by employing any one perspective alone.

While the content of what is taught can be used as a source for reflection, so too can the explicit and implicit knowledge obtained through experience as a program instructor. However, additions to one's store of knowledge through these various ways is insufficient for learning through reflection. Adult and continuing educators must also be committed to using what is learned for reflection on and in practice.

Organizational Learning. Personal, responsive, and reflective learning can also contribute to another kind of learning—organizational learning, or the collective learning by members of the organization. If organizational learning is to occur, however, adult and continuing educators must acknowledge two things. First, they must recognize the importance of understanding how organizations learn and the different forms that organizational learning can take. Second, they must recognize that because they are the ones who are learning from teaching, they are essential agents in effecting any organizational learning that can be derived from their experience as teachers.

According to Argyris and Schön (1978), organizational learning can take two forms: single loop and double loop. In single-loop learning, actions and outcomes are judged against existing organizational standards and norms. When discrepancies are identified, actions can be taken to correct the situation. In this way, single-loop learning functions like a thermostat, detecting deviations from the established norm (the temperature that is set) and acting to bring deviations back in line with that norm (turning on the furnace to raise the temperature to the preestablished level). By teaching in their own units, continuing educators clearly place themselves in a strategic position for uncovering deviations from what is expected in their offices' work with instructors. For example, if, as an instructor, one does not receive information in a timely fashion about travel arrangements for teaching off campus or about availability of instructional resources in the company's library, deficiencies in the office's performance are uncovered and can be corrected.

The type of leadership to which this form of organizational learning primarily contributes is concerned basically with ensuring that performance meets existing standards and norms. Because single-loop learning is constrained by these standards, the type of learning that results and the form of leadership to which it can contribute are therefore likewise limited.

In fact, some would argue that single-loop learning actually relates not to leadership, which is concerned, in one view, with doing the right thing, but rather to management, which is concerned with doing things right (Bennis and Nanus, 1985).

However, what administrators learn from and through teaching also generates rich possibilities for double-loop learning. Double-loop learning differs from single-loop learning in the addition of a loop to the process. In this additional loop, existing assumptions, norms, and standards are brought into question and evaluated in terms of their relevance and appropriateness. If this evaluation finds the assumptions, norms, and standards deficient, then these are modified before actions and outcomes are evaluated with them. In this case, the temperature level of the thermostat is changed, thereby changing the standard with which room temperature is judged.

By shifting roles from administrator to instructor, adult and continuing educators have the opportunity to see their operations from new perspectives, whether gained from the content that they teach or by experiencing their programs as instructors experience them. The development of a deeper understanding about how continuing education students perceive the continuing education office and its programs provides yet another basis on which the appropriateness and relevance of the continuing education unit's assumptions, norms, and standards can be evaluated. As noted earlier, these new and different perspectives create a productive tension with preexisting ideas. As a result, they have much potential for unfreezing administrators' views of existing assumptions and norms and providing insight about how these assumptions and norms can be changed.

Double-loop learning has potential for contributing to transformational leadership, or that form of leadership characterized by attention to ideals and moral values (Burns, 1978), empowerment of others, change, and vision (Bennis and Nanus, 1985). This contribution is possible because in double-loop learning individuals dare to question the basic assumptions, norms, and aims of the organization and its members; they are willing to explore constraints on individual and organizational action; and they seek to transform the organization in light of the vision and values that result from the learning.

For adult and continuing education organizations to learn from teaching, administrators must share what they have learned with other members of the administrative team. According to Senge (1990), teams, not individuals, are the fundamental learning unit in organizations. The learning that the individual administrator obtains from teaching must, therefore, become part of the information with which all staff in the continuing education office work, so that corrections can be made in operations and organizational norms and assumptions can be tested against contrasting viewpoints, whether expressed in course content or by those outside the administrative subculture.

Organizational learning also calls for a particular form of agency by leaders: They are asked to again be teachers (Senge, 1990), but in this case they are responsible for helping the adults *within* their organizations learn. They must not only learn from their teaching experiences but also share with their colleagues the new and different perspectives that they have gained. They must also help their colleagues explicitly deal with the organizational norms and assumptions that they tacitly hold so that these can be analyzed and tested against contrasting viewpoints. In this respect, leaders as teachers help their colleagues focus on the fundamental aims and purposes of the adult and continuing education unit and see the bigger picture of which they and their work are a part (Senge, 1990; Watkins, 1991). Leaders help their colleagues come to truly know their programs, as they themselves have come to know them, adding dimensions of knowing that go beyond knowledge of programs from a strictly managerial perspective.

Conclusion

Cervero (1989) points out that the primary responsibility for improving practice, and therefore for improving leadership, in work settings falls to adult and continuing educators themselves. The major strategy that he recommends is for continuing educators to be researchers of their own practice, so that they can uncover their practical knowledge and understand how they use it on a day-to-day basis.

Teaching provides an important means for continuing educators to research their practice. As has been illustrated, instructional preparation provides hurried administrators with time to reflect on practice. Teaching also affords a means not only for reflecting on one's existing knowledge but also for adding to that store of knowledge perspectives that differ from those contained in the conventional envelope of leadership. Evolving as they do from the complexity and richness of human activity and meaning embedded in programs, these different perspectives open and reconfigure the conventional leadership envelope, allowing leaders and organizations alike to know their programs in ways more profound than those afforded by exclusively managerial perspectives. Having been reconfigured, the envelope allows leaders to be teachers too, providing them with the understanding needed to contribute in more insightful ways to the learning of adults, whether students enrolled in their programs or members of the administrative team for whom they are responsible. Leading as teaching integrates leaders' actions with the educational aims and purposes to which adult and continuing education leadership should be directed.

References

Apps, J. W. *Improving Practice in Continuing Education: Modern Approaches for Understanding the Field and Determining Priorities.* San Francisco: Jossey-Bass, 1985.

Argyris, C., and Schön, D. A. *Organizational Learning: A Theory of Action Perspective.* Reading, Mass.: Addison-Wesley, 1978.

Baden, C. (ed.). *Competitive Strategies for Continuing Education.* New Directions for Adult and Continuing Education, no. 35. San Francisco: Jossey-Bass, 1987.

Bandura, A. *Social Foundations of Thought and Action: A Social-Cognitive Theory.* Englewood Cliffs, N.J.: Prentice Hall, 1986.

Bennis, W. G., and Nanus, B. *Leaders: The Strategies for Taking Charge.* New York: Harper-Collins, 1985.

Burns, J. M. *Leadership.* New York: HarperCollins, 1978.

Cell, E. *Learning to Learn from Experience.* Albany: State University of New York Press, 1984.

Cervero, R. M. *Effective Continuing Education for Professionals.* San Francisco: Jossey-Bass, 1988.

Cervero, R. M. "Becoming More Effective in Everyday Practice." In B. A. Quigley (ed.), *Fulfilling the Promise of Adult and Continuing Education.* New Directions for Adult and Continuing Education, no. 44. San Francisco: Jossey-Bass, 1989.

Courtenay, B. C. "An Analysis of Adult Education Administration Literature, 1936–1989." *Adult Education Quarterly,* 1990, *40* (2), 63–74.

Donaldson, J. F. *Managing Credit Programs in Continuing Higher Education.* Urbana: Office of Continuing Education and Public Service, University of Illinois, 1990.

Edelson, P. J. "Transitions: Research on the Success of Newer Deans and Directors of Continuing Education." Paper presented at the annual meeting of the National University Continuing Education Association, Miami, Florida, April 20–23, 1991. (ED 336 542)

Edelson, P. J. "Teaching and Total Quality Management in Continuing Education." Paper presented at the annual meeting of the National University Continuing Education Association, San Diego, April 11, 1992.

English, J. K. "Defining the Continuing Education Professional." *Journal of Continuing Higher Education,* 1992, *40* (2), 30–37.

Hentschel, D. "Paths Toward Leadership." In *A Handbook for Professional Development in Continuing Higher Education.* Washington, D.C.: National University Continuing Education Association, 1990.

Katz, D., and Kahn, R. L. *The Social Psychology of Organizations.* (2nd ed.) New York: Wiley, 1978.

Knox, A. B. "Leadership Challenges to Continuing Higher Education." *Journal of Higher Education Management,* 1987, *2* (2), 1–14.

Lewis, L., and Dowling, L. "Meaning Making and Reflective Practice." *Adult Learning,* 1992, *3* (4), 7.

Merton, R. K. *Social Theory and Social Science.* (3rd ed.) New York: Free Press, 1968.

Mezirow, J., and Associates. *Fostering Critical Reflection in Adulthood: A Guide to Transformative and Emancipatory Learning.* San Francisco: Jossey-Bass, 1990.

National University Continuing Education Association. *The Next Generation Survey.* Washington, D.C.: National University Continuing Education Association, 1990.

Schein, E. H. *Organizational Culture and Leadership: A Dynamic View.* San Francisco: Jossey-Bass, 1985.

Schön, D. A. *Educating the Reflective Practitioner: Toward a New Design for Teaching and Learning in the Professions.* San Francisco: Jossey-Bass, 1987.

Senge, P. M. *The Fifth Discipline: The Art and Practice of the Learning Organization.* New York: Doubleday/Currency, 1990.

Shipp, T. "The HRD Professional: A Macromotion Study." In W. M. Rivera and S. W. Walker (comps.), *Proceedings of the Lifelong Learning Research Conference.* College Park, Md.: Department of Agriculture and Extension Education, University of Maryland, 1985.

Simerly, R. G., and Associates. *Strategic Planning and Leadership in Continuing Education: Enhancing Organizational Vitality, Responsiveness, and Identity.* San Francisco: Jossey-Bass, 1987.

Van Maanen, J., and Barley, S. R. "Occupational Communities: Culture and Control in Organizations." *Research in Organizational Behavior,* 1984, *6,* 287–365.

Watkins, K. E. "Many Voices: Defining Human Resource Development from Different Disciplines." *Adult Education Quarterly,* 1991, *41* (4), 241–255.

Yule, D.L.G. "Management of Learning in Work Settings." Unpublished doctoral dissertation, Department of Adult Education, Ontario Institute for Studies in Education, University of Toronto, 1979.

JOE F. DONALDSON *is associate professor of higher and adult education, University of Missouri, Columbia.*

Daloz's mentorship model for teaching students is applied to administrative settings, where it can be effectively used as an organizing concept for staff development, a critical leadership activity.

Leadership and Staff Development: A Mentorship Model

Laurent A. Parks Daloz, Paul J. Edelson

Although leaders are still often portrayed in the popular imagination as loners, as tough solitary males who prevail against men of lesser stature and imagination, in fact most contemporary studies of leadership indicate that effective leaders, women as well as men, are skilled at working with people. In particular, they care about the welfare of their colleagues and staff, knowing that their own success depends on the success of all engaged in the enterprise. In these times of rapid change, they know also that simply to subsist, they must move ahead; to thrive, they must be capable of growing and developing in accord with (and sometimes opposition to) changes in the larger world. In this chapter, we propose that effective leaders know that they are interdependent with their people and that they must develop together. Effective leaders serve as mentors to their organizations and foster the development of the people within them. What does it mean to "foster development"? To answer that, let us begin with a look at three dimensions of development that might be of value to leaders of adult education programs.

Three Dimensions of Development

A survey of prevailing human development theories suggests at least three important principles for this discussion. First, development is more than either simple maturation from within or response to stimuli from without. To understand development is to understand the *interaction* of both internal and external forces. Both nature and nurture play a part. Second, as both individuals and systems develop, they become more complex and differentiated. They move from relatively simple, monolithic forms given to global, generalized responses, toward the growth of more highly distinct yet integrated parts and functions—a capacity for more differentiated and appropriate responses to the environment. And, third, the developing individuals or organizations grow less and less self-centered as they come to interact more fully in a complex world. Both individual and organizational maturity bring with them the capacity to function collaboratively in the interest of the larger whole rather than solely in a self-protective, competitive, zero-sum game.

How We Look at the Work Environment

Work is a context in which performance and functionality are valued. It is a setting where we are expected to accomplish an identifiable task or tasks, whether the product is amorphous and abstract or concrete and tangible. Productivity is therefore an important concern of leaders, who are usually held responsible for the output of their units, divisions, or organizations. Questions about the effectiveness and productivity of American industry and the American work force have led to the search for more efficient models and the quest for the superperforming organization, the Holy Grail of the late twentieth century.

Ouchi's (1981) study of Japanese business concluded that cumulative, synergistic individual and group commitment was the key to superior productivity. Overlapping and multiple bonds among workers made for a closer identification with the organization. The Japanese workplace was also characterized by more egalitarian relationships among all members of the organization, with less distance between successive levels of employees.

Ouchi's book promoted the understanding and acceptance that, through work, individuals are fulfilling basic and fundamental human needs. Achievement of these social objectives, which were closely associated with being part of a mutually supportive community, contributed to focused productivity and high-quality performance. Ouchi suggested that management could influence the development of social commitment in the workplace. The use of work teams, a consultative form of decision making that seeks to acknowledge and, if possible, incorporate disparate viewpoints, and the promise of lifetime employment, symbolizing management's commitment to the worker in good times and bad, result in a dedicated, high-performance work force.

The task of abstracting from Ouchi's study the concept of mutual commitment and the nurturing of closer, more meaningful relationships among staff presents a challenge to leadership. We are compelled to ask, What do we expect of "work"? In a study of young adults in the M.B.A. program at the Harvard Business school (Parks, 1993), researchers were struck by the growing concern of these "best and brightest" for what they termed *balance*. Noting the ravages of the 1980s on the lives of those ahead of them, the students were becoming increasingly concerned about the personal cost of the tendency to split the realm of work sharply apart from the realm of love. Given the intense competitive pressures of the business world toward which they aspired, these young people worried (with considerable reason) that their family lives could suffer. It should not be a surprise, then, that concurrent with this concern has been a sharp rise in references to mentorship in the workplace. It is as though the system is responding to the threat of impersonalism by expressing its hunger for this new form of personal, caring, human contact in the midst of what appears to many as a wasteland.

Thus, it seems important to consider the workplace as more than simply a locale for producing goods and services, using up time, and generating income. We need to reexamine the socially rewarding aspects of work in addition to whatever personal satisfaction and fulfillment it may offer. For adult and continuing educators in particular, the work environment is more than an area of instrumental productivity. It is real and authentic, an end in itself, affording both a site and means for the evolution of society. We place the work lives of adults, including those who work alongside us in adult education programs, within an educational, developmental context. We view the field of adult education as a representation of the society that we wish to bring about—a society of lifelong learning and lifelong learners.

How We View Staff

How do we actually begin to locate ourselves and staff in this interpretation of the adult and continuing education workplace? When we consider hiring and training, by what means do we look beyond issues of direct functionality toward the developmental needs of staff?

One initial clue may rest in the person's background and the degree to which it indicates a pattern of adult learning. If a person has made deliberate decisions about adult and continuing education, we may learn a lot about the person's values and attitude toward change. Too often, however, employers tend to focus solely on prior work experience as if that revealed the entire person. Yet, this seems little more than a form of technocratic insight, for in today's workplace what matters is not so much the skills and attributes that a person already brings to the job but rather those that they will need to learn and develop. Thus, one critical aspect of mentoring is to promote the use of adult education in this fashion. Our attitude toward people and their capacity to change contributes to the philosophy and values that we emphasize at the work site. These, in turn, circumscribe the application of administrative and technical expertise.

Commitment at Work

The concept of commitment is often cited as a central factor in the employment process. Typically, the reference is to hard work, dedication, and sacrifice beyond what is minimally acceptable for the good of the organization and attainment of its goals. One of us, Laurent Daloz, is part of a team now studying the formation of commitment among those who have worked for many years on behalf of the common good. He has found that central to long-term commitment is a sense of vocation, of a "calling" (which may or may not be religious) to some purpose larger than the individual or tribal self. Those most capable of sustained commitment seem to be those who see their work in the context of community or global concerns and who can balance personal with altruistic needs.

Part of the commitment to staff can include participation in a lifelong learning community that stresses staff development in its broadest, most ambitious, idealistic sense through the practice of adult and continuing education. In this way, employment can become a way of merging personal with professional aspirations.

The Place of Mentorship

Mentorship is often viewed as a solitary business in which one individual shares responsibility for another's developmental journey. Although a venerable human activity, its place in life-span development was first systematically recognized by Levinson (1978) in his landmark study of the lives of forty men. In the business world, Kanter (1977) recognized the importance of what she called a "sponsor," and Roche (1979) described the place of mentorship in organizational development—an important means by which young adults make their way to the top of the corporate ladder. Mentors, it seems, are valuable for both personal and career development. By now, there has been an explosion of books and articles describing the career advantages to those who can find and benefit from a mentor's assistance.

Less attention, however, has been paid to the ways in which mentors actually work to enhance the cognitive and psychological development of their charges, as we have defined development here. In a book directed to teachers and mentors in higher education, Daloz (1986) suggests and applies a mentorship model for the teaching of adults, using the metaphor of a developmental journey and drawing on such mythic figures as Mentor in *The Odyssey* and Virgil in *The Divine Comedy*. Effective mentors, he suggests, have a good, if intuitive, understanding of how they want their protégés to develop, and he offers several such "developmental maps." He goes on to suggest that they nudge their charges on their way by a complex blend of three elements: support, challenge, and vision. That is, they create a climate of trust in which the learner feels safe to risk taking new perspectives, they introduce tension by raising disorienting questions or setting tasks, and they offer direction and vision by suggesting the larger dimensions of the task on which the learner is embarking.

In the remainder of this chapter, we propose a way in which this expanded notion of mentorship can be transplanted into the work setting so that mentors may be seen not simply as conductors on the fast track but also, in a deeper sense, as guides on a journey toward something like wisdom, a journey that, as Virgil knew, may well lead down before it leads up.

Staff Development and Five Key Steps of Mentoring

One popular view of staff development is simply the hiring of competent, experienced people who then practice within their new institutional settings. In effect, we engage semi-independent professionals who already know what they should be doing. We then provide resources and autonomy. Additional training and development decisions, when necessary, are made directly by the individuals, who are motivated by socially constructed and internalized concepts of professionalism.

Another view of staff development is more prescriptive. What do we as organizational leaders want that staff person to accomplish? Is the person skilled enough to achieve the necessary objectives? A top-down view of organizational purposes and then of training needs becomes de rigueur if staff are viewed as inadequately prepared to participate in the task of setting organizational goals.

Mentoring requires changes in the relationships among staff members, compelling higher management to become more directly involved in reciprocal relationships. It requires participation in relationships characterized by intersubjectivity in which colleagues share their perspectives of individual tasks as well as of larger all-encompassing organizational goals. Contrasted with the laissez-faire and prescriptive approaches to staff development, mentoring requires an individual not only to take responsibility for staff development but also to let go, allowing both parties to shape processes and outcomes. What are the implications of what we know about how effective mentors function for the creation of an institutionwide mentoring environment for staff development?

Engender Trust. A primary condition for the optimal development of the individual is basic trust (Erikson, 1950). Experienced mentors know that growth invariably entails a significant degree of risk and that if the relationship with their protégés is not characterized by trust and honesty, the potential of the partnership will be compromised. Likewise, if an organization is to grow—better, not simply bigger—and if it is to foster the development of the individuals under its wing, management is well advised to create conditions under which the staff members feel safe to experiment, risk, and participate as fully as possible in the growth of the organization as well as in their own growth.

Thus, management must understand that freedom to fail is a precondition for growth and that a primary task of a mentoring environment is to create a safe space for the development of competence. Adult and continuing education deans and directors should provide a safety net for failure by building the element of experimentation into all jobs. To do this, they must embrace the notion that there is no one best way, only changing solutions to changing problems. It is unrealistic to expect people to push at the margins of their performance envelopes if leadership is itself fearful of change or failure.

Understand the Student's Movement in a Developmental Framework. Effective mentorship entails more than the simple feeding of information to the student or random support. There is a direction to development; growth is about movement. Mentors are guides to learners on their journeys. They have a sense of what they want for their students, of where the journey leads. Likewise, effective leaders carry a vision for their organizations; they have at least some sense of how they want to guide their staffs on the enterprise.

Leaders' ideas for the future of organizations are therefore outgrowths of their capacity to maintain confidence in the developmental outcomes of their people. Long-range goals are of necessity vague and are only given meaning by the actions of individuals. The tasks of getting staff members to articulate their own and larger goals, working with them on any necessary skills attainment, and finding areas of mutual convergence with others provide an elastic framework for developmental movement.

Introduce Conflict and Encourage the Student's Voice. An important element of the mentor's art is the willingness to raise questions and challenge the learner at appropriate times. The capacity to address discontinuity and conflict is a crucial part of significant learning. At the same time, this conflict must be carefully calibrated to serve the larger purpose of strengthening, not debilitating, the learner. The effective mentor skillfully balances challenge and support so as to empower the learner's voice. The effective leader likewise encourages and urges his or her people on as they move together in a common direction. According to Heifetz (1992), effective leaders mobilize people to work on their problems. They help their people to frame and name the problems in such a way that the entire organization can perform the adaptive work of changing to meet the emerging need in a productive fashion.

The leader's role in creating conflict and precipitating feelings of uncertainty is a way of moving people into the future. There is a need to make this purpose clear and to show that mild forms of conflict and anxiety are necessary to overcome inertia and the lassitude of the status quo.

Emphasize Positive Movement. With the direction clearly in mind, mentors find ways to remind their protégés of their continuing progress, to help them name those sometimes small shifts toward greater perspective or deeper wisdom that characterize the growth valued by both partners. By encouraging learners to tell and retell their stories, mentors help them to reinvent themselves as they grow into more adequate, richer selves. Likewise, leaders can take advantage of opportunities to tell and share the emerging stories of their own institutions in ways that bring out the ongoing transformation and development of the organizations.

Regardless of magnitude, all positive change is to be celebrated. It is necessary for leaders to look at transformation incrementally and from a cumulative perspective. Successful staff members can serve as models for others, although it must be pointed out that the mentor's goal is not to produce clones but rather to enhance individual development.

Attend to the Relationship. Mentors also know that in an important sense "the journey is home." One must keep house; it is important to attend to the relationship, monitoring not only the protégé's feelings about it but also one's own feelings about it. Just as a growing relationship requires that time and attention be given to the relationship, so also must time and attention be given to the inner health of the organization. Much as the goal for the individual is a well-integrated psyche, the goal of the organization is a well-integrated home in which all members are respected, can speak freely and fully, and can grow to their capacity for continuing relationships.

Organizational goals, especially extrinsic performance measures, need to be placed in proper perspective alongside individual views of success. Adult and continuing educators need to realize that the meaning of education is still a contested subject. Rigor in thought and praxis ought not be sacrificed for an arid rigidity composed of enrollment targets or tuition revenue.

Establishing Mentoring Programs in the Organization

Recent years have brought a number of successful and unsuccessful efforts to establish formal mentoring networks in both private and public organizations. These are described at considerable length by Murray-Hicks (1972), Kram (1985), Fagan (1986), Gray (1986), and Murray (1991). Kram's (1985) analysis of how mentorships in the workplace foster development remains one of the most carefully crafted treatments of the phenomenon. Zey (1986) has persuasively argued that mentoring programs will expand rapidly in the coming years.

Probably the most comprehensive guidelines for such programs appear in Murray's (1991) practical guide, *Beyond the Myths and Magic of Mentoring*. She defines these programs as "a deliberate pairing of a more skilled or experienced person with a lesser skilled or experienced one, with the agreed-upon goal of having the lesser skilled person grow and develop specific competencies" (p. xiv). It is clear from a wide range of research that such programs can be effective means of staff development, and Murray provides numerous examples of their potential benefits. At the same time, she notes a range of problems that frequently arise, including favoritism, gender issues, power confusions, and disenchantment. It is essential, she emphasizes, that organizations contemplating such programs take careful account of their particular configurations of needs, philosophies, and resources to tailor these programs to fit.

Providing Vision

Perhaps the most important function of mentors is that of *providing vision*, of offering the protégés a range of ethically responsible possibilities around which to orient their commitment. The mentor knows that to see the way ahead, it is often valuable to be able to look behind. Thus, in the service of evoking a vision for the future, the wise mentor recalls our history. One of today's leading figures in adult education, Stephen Brookfield (1990), reminds us that the man most often associated with the founding of modern adult education, Eduard Lindeman, knew that the core commitment of adult education was based on a broad vision of social change. Adult education ought to do more, Lindeman maintained, than merely stock the shelves of the corporation with skilled workers. It ought to lead learners to examine the underlying assumptions of their society and to work toward positive social change (Lindeman, 1926). Accordingly, leaders in adult and continuing education have a special call to further Lindeman's vision by serving as mentors to their own staffs and promoting vigorous, imaginative, and effective staff development programs. If we are to take seriously the term staff development, we must do more than teach skills to our staff. We also must direct the development of all involved in adult education toward the realization of a more just society.

References

Brookfield, S. D. "Expanding Knowledge About How We Learn." In R. Smith and Associates, *Learning to Learn Across the Lifespan*. San Francisco: Jossey-Bass, 1990.

Daloz, L. A. *Effective Teaching and Mentoring: Realizing the Transformational Power of Adult Learning Experiences*. San Francisco: Jossey-Bass, 1986.

Erikson, E. *Childhood and Society*. New York: Norton, 1950.

Fagan, M. "Do Formal Mentoring Programs Really Mentor?" In *Proceedings of the First International Conference on Mentoring*. Vol. 2. Vancouver, British Columbia, Canada: International Association for Mentoring, 1986.

Gray, W. "Developing a Planned Mentoring Program to Facilitate Career Development." *International Journal of Mentoring*, 1986, 2 (1).

Heifetz, R. "To Lead or Mislead? The Challenge of Adaptive Change." Unpublished manuscript, John F. Kennedy School of Government, Harvard University, 1992.

Kanter, R. M. *Men and Women of the Corporation.* New York: Basic Books, 1977.

Kram, K. *Mentoring at Work: Developmental Relationships in Organizational Life.* Glenview, Ill.: Scott Foresman, 1985.

Levinson, D. *Seasons of a Man's Life.* New York: Knopf, 1978.

Lindeman, E. *The Meaning of Adult Education.* New York: New Republic, 1926.

Murray, M. *Beyond the Myths and Magic of Mentoring: How to Facilitate an Effective Mentoring Program.* San Francisco: Jossey-Bass, 1991.

Murray-Hicks, M. *Generic Model for a Facilitated Mentoring Program.* Oakland, Calif.: Managers' Mentors, 1972.

Ouchi, W. G. *Theory Z.* New York: Avon Books, 1981.

Parks, S. "Is It too Late?" In T. Piper, M. Gentile, and S. Parks (eds.), *Can Ethics Be Taught?* Boston: Harvard Business School Press, 1993.

Roche, G. "Much Ado About Mentors." *Harvard Business Review,* 1979, *20,* 14–18.

Zey, M. "Only the Beginning: Five Major Trends That Signal the Growth of Corporate Formal Mentor Programs." In *Proceedings of the First International Conference on Mentoring.* Vol. 2. Vancouver, British Columbia, Canada: International Association for Mentoring, 1986.

LAURENT A. PARKS DALOZ currently serves as a mentor for adults at Lesley College, Cambridge, Massachusetts. He is also coresearcher in a national study of the lives of people committed to work on behalf of the common good.

PAUL J. EDELSON is dean of the School of Continuing Education and director of the Continuing Education Research Center at the State University of New York, Stony Brook.

An increasingly pluralistic higher education environment demands that its leadership acknowledge, understand, and guide the new and emerging values and beliefs that are reshaping institutional culture.

Symbolic Leadership: Redefining Relations with the Host Organization

Judith L. McGaughey

The attributes that define effective leadership are increasingly difficult to identify and classify as organizational entities become larger, more complex, and more diverse. In this chapter, I look at the role of leadership in adult and continuing education as it exists in the larger host organization. The framework for discussion is the urban community college, though its applicability to other institutional settings is evident. Particular attention is given here to the role of the adult and continuing education head as a symbolic leader, a leader who frames and reinforces the values and beliefs that define the culture of the continuing education unit.

Demographics and the Changing Institutional Culture

The urban community college has grown dramatically in the past decade. With this growth have come increasingly diverse student and staff populations. Especially in urban areas, changing demographics of communities (more Asians and Hispanics, for example) have been reflected in the populations enrolling in community colleges. Increasing numbers of women are returning to school and find the community college especially accessible. As urban and suburban populations shift from predominantly white residents to increasing numbers of Hispanic, African American, and Asian ethnic groups, these demographic changes are reflected in the enrollments of community colleges. Accompanying this ethnic diversity is an increasingly pluralistic culture. These different ethnic groups of students are diverse in educational backgrounds, economic situations, cultural experiences, and expectations, which means that the previously established institutional culture must undergo dramatic shifts. It is critical that the leadership in such institutions recognize the shift in student populations and how this shift ultimately changes the institutional culture.

Culture-driven institutional policies based on a predominantly white student and staff population may denigrate the integrity and worth of certain new groups now entering community colleges. As Bensimon, Newmann, and Birnbaum (1989) point out, institutional culture is difficult to modify intentionally, and organizational size and complexity often work against accommodation of the distinctive patterns of values and assumptions of different subpopulations of students. Given this reality, the new pluralistic culture must consider multiple definitions of effective leadership and multiple measures of institutional success. Large institutions tend to establish all-encompassing policies and operational procedures in order to make the institution more manageable and cost-effective. These universal standards may not mesh with the needs and expectations of distinctive groups of staff and students. Thus, in order to establish policies and procedures that respond to both institutional and client needs, the institution must become more pluralistic in its programs and perspectives.

As recent writings suggest, the traditional, anticipated goals of students enrolled in postsecondary institutions are changing, especially in community colleges. The historical expectation of student outcomes in the college or university system has been the attainment of a college degree. Patterns of student enrollment in community colleges increasingly indicate that degrees are not the primary objectives for many students. Students move in and out of a structured college experience as their personal and employment needs dictate. Adelman (1992) concludes that community colleges accommodate students in their decisions to learn on their own terms and in their own time. He also notes that the community colleges play only a small role in credentialing students or in determining their occupational outcomes. Thus, an increasingly diverse student population is creating a more pluralistic institutional culture, which in turn is leading to a broader range of student outcomes.

The American community college has traditionally been based on three overarching premises: the colleges' openness to the entire adult population, the colleges' rootedness in the communities in which they are located, and the colleges' willingness to deviate from more traditional academic patterns (Brint and Karabel, 1989). The institutional mission is generally developed out of these premises, identifying the comprehensive purpose of the college, its relationship to academic and career programs, and the college's service to the community. The college's mission may need to be revisited. Does it reflect the increasing diversity of its student population and the communities from which these students come?

The Postsecondary Institution as an Organizational Entity

Whether we are looking at a university, a four-year or two-year college, or a continuing education unit, it is useful to view these settings from an organizational perspective. Every organization looks to establish and perform its particular mission. Bolman and Deal (1984) provide a framework for viewing organizations that highlights four perspectives: (1) structural, which emphasizes formal roles and relationships; (2) human resources, which focuses on the needs of the people in the organization; (3) political, which focuses on the competition for existing resources; and (4) symbolic, which views the organization as a culture with shared values. Bolman and Deal suggest that good leaders must have a comprehensive understanding of all four perspectives.

A structural perspective highlights the leader's role in making decisions and in designing systems of control and coordination that direct the work of others (Bensimon, Newmann, and Birnbaum, 1989). Most leadership studies suggest that good leaders are generally good decision makers regardless of the organizational setting. From a human resources perspective, most effective leaders grapple with the complex interactions among people at all levels of the institution and recognize the importance of communication in the making of decisions and the accomplishment of tasks leading to desired outcomes. The political arena is also well established, with various sectors of the institution often negotiating and competing for existing personnel, fiscal, and facility resources. Again, in institutions that are generally considered productive and committed to achieving certain goals, the quality of leadership can usually be measured from these three perspectives.

What is more difficult to assess is the symbolic perspective, from which leadership must increasingly be viewed in the context of a dramatically changing institutional culture. As the organization becomes increasingly pluralistic, the task of identifying shared values becomes much more complex. Recent studies suggest that transforming leadership and interpretive leadership are the two types of leadership most able to adapt to rapidly changing institutional cultures.

As Bensimon, Newmann, and Birnbaum (1989) indicate, leaders who understand the symbolic perspective are usually catalysts or facilitators of an ongoing process. Such leaders no longer look at the institutional mission as necessarily one only of product but, equally important, as one of process. Green (1988) indicates that the transforming leader must encourage the college community to accept a vision created and maintained through the leader's symbolic actions. These actions serve to shape the values, symbols, and emotions that influence the behaviors of individuals (Bensimon, Newmann, and Birnbaum, 1989). For example, a prior institutional value espoused by the leader may be that standardized test grades are the most important measures of student success. The transforming leader may suggest other values (such as portfolio review or oral interview) as more important measures. In another instance, leaders, through their actions, may stress consensus as an important value for decision making. Transforming leaders recognize that in different situations and with changing institutional constituencies, values shift. Again, the institutional reality is one of process, not only product.

Leadership in Adult and Continuing Education

Let us now look at symbolic leadership in relation to adult and continuing education. Educators frequently state that adult and continuing education is often an ancillary or marginal function of the host organization. But this statement is becoming less true, especially in urban community college settings. Among the various college units, the adult and continuing education program has often been the first to respond to the changing demographics of the local community. *Access* is the watchword of adult and continuing education programs that take root in community locations and encourage new groups of adults to participate in postsecondary education.

This encouragement to participate has drawn especially positive response from minority members of the community, various disenfranchised populations, as well as various special populations (for example, adults with disabilities, people on public assistance, the unemployed and underemployed, and people currently housed in various institutional settings). Adult and continuing education staff have developed education programs to meet specific needs of these groups (for example, programs initiated under the federal Family Support Act of 1988, which mandates education and training to move people from welfare to work). Based on involvement with these populations, the adult and continuing education entity has struggled, usually sooner than the host organization, with changes in student requirements. These diverse groups of students have brought a wide array of education needs and expectations based on distinctive past histories and experiences.

The adult and continuing education unit may be better able than the host organization to adapt to the changing culture because its structures are often more flexible. There also may be fewer institutional rules and regulations to constrain the educational response to student needs. Credentialing may not be a major goal of continuing education, and the range of external organizations with which continuing education interacts creates diverse delivery systems that provide a wide range of options for students.

Increasingly, external agencies are pooling resources to provide a more effective range of services for adults who want and need further education.

For example, the state education department may allocate funds for literacy education that are supplemented by funding from the U.S. Department of Labor to support skills training and job placement. At the same time, the state social services department may provide funding for carfare and child care for their client base enrolled in two-year college programs. This diversity in delivery systems and programs means that adult and continuing education leaders have often been the first to face and overcome the challenges and dilemmas of establishing missions designed for a pluralistic community culture.

As White and Belt (1980) indicate, experienced professionals in adult and continuing education are usually self-initiating, growth oriented, creative, and energetic. These professionals work long hours and handle a vast array of problems, often without full institutional authority to do so. For example, the warden of a local jail, where college classes are held, may terminate classes because of inmate disruptions. The continuing education leader may then intercede with the corrections commissioner to reinstitute classes. Thus, a new role for the leader is born.

The adult and continuing education leaders' influence beyond their direct spheres of authority may be less than that of the more traditional administrators at comparable rank and level elsewhere in the organization. As White and Belt (1980) suggest, because of this lesser power base, persuasion and influence become more important ingredients in effective leadership of adult and continuing education entities. The need for dynamic leadership in adult and continuing education may also be more critical than exists in other areas because of the heavy reliance on shifting fiscal resources, large numbers of part-time faculty, and fragile and complex relationships with external agencies. Such relationships are often critical to programmatic success because these agencies exercise significant legislative, political, and economic influence.

Adult and Continuing Education Values

As Bowen (1980) points out, important components of academic leadership include clarity of purpose, dedication, sense of community, love of learning and teaching, personal interest in students, and prudent administration. These qualities may well form the framework in which the adult and continuing education leader becomes the interpreter and reinforcer of the beliefs and values of those involved in adult and continuing education. Bensimon, Newmann, and Birnbaum (1989) suggest that a theory of symbolic leadership focuses on the influence of the leader in maintaining or reinterpreting a system of shared beliefs and values that give meaning to organizational life.

When we look at the culture of the adult and continuing education division, we are looking at its dominant values, norms, philosophy, rules, and climate (Bensimon, Newmann, and Birnbaum, 1989). These should reflect the basic conceptions that the organizational participants (in this case, the adult and continuing education staff) have of themselves and their environment. The leader is expected to mold the culture by creating new symbols and by establishing and reinforcing consistent values. In this way, participants make a greater commitment to the organization and their motivation toward organizational excellence is increased (Bensimon, Newmann, and Birnbaum, 1989).

In the following subsections, I highlight the values and beliefs that, in my experience, are important to adult and continuing education success in a large institutional setting. The values are identified along with specific examples of how they have been realized in the adult and continuing education unit.

Belief in the Educational Potential of Adult Learners Who Have Not Traditionally Had Access to Postsecondary Education. All adult students desiring further education are welcomed to the unit of adult and continuing education. Through counseling and educational assessment, students are referred either to existing programs within continuing education or to other programs in other settings with similar beliefs in the students' educational potential. In most instances, students served in this capacity would not otherwise have an opportunity to enter postsecondary education. Staff must believe in the potential of these students to achieve and be willing to help them develop the best means for accomplishing their goals. It is the responsibility of leadership to support this belief through the allocation of resources as well as through the conception and development of programs that can effectively serve these adult learners.

Dedication to the Goals of Adult and Continuing Education. Not only should there be an institutional mission that guides the host organization, there also should be a mission statement for the adult and continuing education unit. In my institution, LaGuardia Community College, the mission statement addresses the needs of adult learners who would not normally have access to higher education through a broad array of programs and services. In order to accomplish this mission, the Division of Adult and Continuing Education undergoes an annual goal-setting process. Goals and objectives are developed within each program unit of the larger division. Along with goal identification, a time frame is determined for meeting the goals, and required resources are sought for accomplishing the goals. These goals and objectives are then compiled in a divisionwide document, which is circulated for input across all program units. Once this document has been developed in draft form, divisional leaders assess the capacity to meet the goals based on existing and projected financial, staff, and facility resources. A final document is prepared that reflects the priorities established by staff in individual program units. Goals are reviewed at midyear for potential revision based on progress at that point.

At academic year's end, goals are again revisited within program units as well as across the Division of Adult and Continuing Education. This review forms the basis for the development of the next year's goals.

Hard Work. There is no substitute for hard work in the accomplishment of goals within continuing education. This means hard work by the leadership as well as the staff and students. There are no time clocks or lock-in schedules for staff. There is an institutional climate that assumes the needs of students are such that they require no less than long hours and dedication. Staff are generally free to establish a work schedule that matches the instructional program. Ninety percent of the time, this means more than a thirty-five-hour work week. Although there is no formal way to acknowledge time given above and beyond the call of duty, individual program units are allowed to determine when the pace can be eased and staff schedules adjusted.

Students also work extremely hard. They work at jobs, they work in their roles as parents and as community residents, and they work at school. These multiple roles are fully acknowledged in the content and philosophy of continuing education programs. Curricula are specifically created to encompass the students' roles as workers, parents, and citizens. Since many students have not engaged in formal education for some time, orientation and counseling are provided to enhance participant self-esteem and to reintroduce students to the rigors of academic achievement. Support services are provided as needed, including tutoring, child care, and transportation.

Staff have high standards for students, and students therefore set high standards for themselves. Although there are moments of frustration when goals cannot be accomplished in the time initially anticipated, longer-term goals likely allow the student to become more successful in his or her varied roles.

Consistency. Staff have the right to know what to expect from their leaders, and, similarly, students have a right to know what to expect from the instructional and support staff with whom they interact. Such consistency is especially critical in the adult and continuing education unit because so many of the influences (funding support, economic conditions, public policy) that relate to program activity and outcome fluctuate and are extremely variable. The leaders must be consistent and clear in the values that they espouse, in their expectations of staff behaviors, and in identifying priorities. Only in this way can staff have assurance that their efforts will be supported.

Although there is never a dull moment in continuing education and new programs are constantly being developed, work is not accomplished chaotically. There is consistency in the pattern of activity. Administrators have regular supervisory meetings with program staff. Every program unit generates periodic activity and outcome reports. Payroll procedures, staff evaluations, and supply and equipment acquisitions follow standard procedures and apply to all programs.

Professionalism. This term refers to competence of performance, which leads to excellence. The leader behaves professionally in speaking, in writing, in assessing, and in doing. This level of commitment to competence is also expected of staff and students. A high level of competence establishes the reputation of the continuing education enterprise and spills over to the host organization as well. Sloppiness in writing or thinking should not be acceptable. Inattention to detail, inaccuracy in assessment, and less than full attention to service delivery to students should not be condoned.

The need for such high standards is especially critical when viewed in the context of the needs of most adult learners now engaged in continuing education. Given the growing gap between the skills of today's students and the technological demands of the workplace, doing less than our best is insufficient. The increasing gap, politically and economically, between the haves and have-nots, as well as society's ineffectual response to the breakdown of families and growing social unrest, put great responsibility on the education system to assist in ameliorating these conditions. The continuing education leaders can ask no less of themselves than they do of those with whom they interact: staff, colleagues, students, and external constituencies.

Integrity. The value of integrity is viewed both personally and professionally. This encompasses total sincerity and honesty in philosophy and approach to policy and practice in adult and continuing education. Programs without integrity cannot effectively prepare adults for the critical demands that they face in their roles as workers, parents, and responsible citizens. Likewise, staff who do not exhibit a fundamental personal integrity in their beliefs cannot be positive role models for students. An honest approach to learning and accomplishments transcends individual differences of background, culture, and social persuasion.

Diversity as a Positive Attribute. Not until the dominant cultural and ethnic groups have fuller interaction with newly arriving groups with their own distinctive cultures will prejudices and stereotypes be reduced. The education environment should provide a positive locus for this interaction across cultures. This dialogue should occur at all organizational levels. By working and thinking together, staff and students may gain fuller and more accurate understandings of the values and beliefs of different individuals and groups of individuals. Through this interaction, the positive value of diversity emerges. There is greater understanding of multiple points of view directed toward a particular issue or problem. This creates an atmosphere of greater acceptance of different attitudes and perspectives. Issues of diversity and pluralism must be explored in an atmosphere of mutual respect and trust in outcomes. Although difficult, leaders must be willing to be challenged and to witness confrontation. They must be able to face negative confrontation and stimulate processes that lead to positive and mutually supporting outcomes. If leaders are not willing to take this risk, then neither can staff or students.

Credit and Noncredit Distinctions May Not Be Meaningful Measures of Educational Accomplishment. One of the reasons that continuing education has been viewed both internally and externally as a marginal or ancillary activity is the belief that noncredit learning is less valuable than credit learning. Adult students have helped us redefine what real learning is all about. This real learning has little relationship to credits earned. It has a much stronger relationship to skills needed on a job, attributes that make parenting a more positive reality, and cognitive skills development that helps individuals better understand the conflicts and problems faced both personally and professionally. As students have helped continuing educators relearn the value of learning, the continuing educator has become less the victim of this dichotomous thinking about credit and noncredit activity. It is incumbent on adult and continuing education leaders to ensure that this understanding goes beyond the continuing education unit. The devaluation of noncredit learning is inimical to the great educational strides made by learners in continuing education programs.

Commitment to Lifelong Learning for Oneself and One's Students. As most adult educators are aware, lifelong learning occurs in many ways and in many situations. It can be self-directed or instructor-driven, it can take place in unstructured as well as structured settings, and it may occur intermittently or regularly. What is common to the pattern of lifelong learning is the intent of the individual to learn something new, to discover something beyond current knowledge and understanding. Adult and continuing education leaders should not only espouse the significance of lifelong learning but also act as models. Our own lifelong learning experiences have both ritual and substantive value in this context. The ritual value is that we have engaged in structured and unstructured learning activity. The substantive value is that we have hopefully gained in knowledge, appreciation, and understanding in some new facet of thinking or experience.

The above values and beliefs have proved to be important attributes of the culture of adult and continuing education. This culture is pluralistic and diverse by virtue of its staff, students, and programs. Amidst this diversity, it is possible to establish certain common values and beliefs that provide the framework for successful educational experience and accomplishment by the adult learner.

Relationship to the Host Organization

The next critical step for the adult and continuing education leader is to carry this vision to the larger host organization and thereby contribute to the larger institutional culture. The adult and continuing education leader can also share certain outcomes derived from the unit's values and beliefs. To reinforce the belief in the educational potential of the continuing education student, the leader can share student success stories with the host organization and with external audiences.

The adult and continuing education goals document should be shared with other institutional leaders. At the least, it can increase external leaders' knowledge of continuing education. At best, the goals process may become a model for similar processes in other institutional units.

Purposeful hard work by continuing education leaders in the larger organization can expand their influence in the host organization. Increasingly, host organizations are called on to develop stronger linkages and affiliations with external agencies. The experiences of the adult and continuing education unit, which has had to develop such relationships for survival, can now be useful in the host organization's attempts to establish the same kinds of linkages.

A positive reputation, developed through hard work and professionalism in adult and continuing education, redounds to the larger institution. It is often the continuing education unit that has established the strongest ties to the community. This linkage paves the way for other collaborative arrangements. It is unlikely that other institutional leaders will want to diminish the positive reputation but will instead want to build on it.

The adult and continuing education unit and the leader's integrity may be vulnerable if the host organization views continuing education only in the context of its role as the "cash cow." Such emphasis on economic outcomes can corrupt the philosophy and mission of continuing education. It is essential that the adult and continuing education leader continually emphasize the substantive importance of the unit's programs to the host organization and the larger community. The adult and continuing education unit cannot afford to be a financial drain on the organization, but its financial role should not be paramount. The adult and continuing education leader must be adept in fiscal management so that the most pressing education needs can be met without damaging the institution's financial base. This should not be done at the expense of a coherent mission.

Although the larger institution may not have a specific understanding of the needs of the adult learner or of the importance of lifelong learning, the adult and continuing education leader can share information and outcomes in order to enhance the knowledge base of leaders in the larger institutional setting.

Very often the goals of adult and continuing education parallel and even enhance goals of the larger institution. Where these parallels exist, this information should be communicated to the leadership of the larger organization. For example, the creation of new continuing education programs can act as feeder programs to degree study, thus increasing institutional enrollments. Likewise, examples of adult student success in noncredit programs should be recognized and praised in settings beyond the adult and continuing education unit. As the activities and objectives of the adult and continuing education division have become more complex and diverse, the measures of these accomplishments have also become more complicated. This reality should be recognized in the larger organizational setting. Although there will continue to be distinctions in purpose and outcomes, there should be universal understanding that everyone as an educator hopes to advance the skills and knowledge of the participant learners.

Conclusion

Leadership is a product of opportunity, training, initiative, and instincts that creatively adapt an institution to its environment (Alfred, Elsner, and LeCroy, 1984). Since we know the environment is changing dramatically, especially in urban areas, leadership becomes more a process than a product. It will become increasingly important for leaders in adult and continuing education as well as leaders in the larger organizational setting to be able to interpret the roles and missions of their respective entities within the local education delivery system. At the same time, leaders must maintain balance and perspective in setting priorities, managing scarce resources, and encouraging vision beyond the immediate social and economic conditions.

In adult and continuing education and in the larger organizational setting, there should be a strong commitment to the goal of excellence in programs and services. As McCabe (1984) has suggested, community college leaders must maintain a broad perspective on issues. Certainly, the president must be a visionary and must keep the focus directed on the essential purposes and values of the institution. I suggest, in a similar fashion, that adult and continuing education leaders must continue to focus on the essential purpose, mission, and values of adult and continuing education in relation to both the learner and the host organization.

Although the effective leader will necessarily have good problem-solving, decision-making, and communication skills, this may not be sufficient in the growing complexity and diversity of higher education institutions. What will become the critical next ingredient is a fuller understanding of the culture in which decisions are made, issues addressed, and education goals accomplished. Institutional culture is changing dramatically with shifts in community demographics and new larger societal needs at home, in the workplace, and in the community. Symbolic leadership will have a guiding influence in understanding and shaping an increasingly pluralistic institutional culture in higher education.

References

Adelman, C. *The Way We Are: The Community College as American Thermometer.* Washington, D.C.: Government Printing Office, 1992.

Alfred, R., Elsner, P., and LeCroy, J. (eds.). *Emerging Roles for Community College Leaders.* New Directions for Community Colleges, no. 46. San Francisco: Jossey-Bass, 1984.

Bensimon, E., Newmann, A., and Birnbaum, R. *Making Sense of Administrative Leadership: The "L" Word in Higher Education.* ASHE-ERIC Higher Education Reports, no. 1. Washington, D.C.: Association for the Study of Higher Education, 1989.

Bolman, L. G., and Deal, T. E. *Modern Approaches to Understanding and Managing Organizations.* San Francisco: Jossey-Bass, 1984.

Bowen, H. R. *The Costs of Higher Education: How Much Do Colleges and Universities Spend Per Student and How Much Should They Spend?* San Francisco: Jossey-Bass, 1980.

Brint, S., and Karabel, J. *The Diverted Dream: Community Colleges and the Promise of Educational Opportunity in America, 1900–1985.* New York: Oxford University Press, 1989.

Green, M. F. (ed.). *Leaders for a New Era: Strategies for Higher Education.* New York: American Council on Education/Macmillan, 1988.

McCabe, R. H. "Dimensions of Change Confronting Institutional Leaders." In R. Alfred, P. Elsner, and R. LeCroy (eds.), *Emerging Roles for Community College Leaders.* New Directions for Community Colleges, no. 46. San Francisco: Jossey-Bass, 1984.

White, T. J., and Belt, J. R. "Leadership." In A. B. Knox and Associates, *Developing, Administering, and Evaluating Adult Education.* San Francisco: Jossey-Bass, 1980.

JUDITH L. MCGAUGHEY is dean of adult and continuing education at LaGuardia Community College of the City University of New York.

*Human resources development professionals can help establish
continuous learning environments for their organizations that have
a profound impact on all employees. Leadership in this realm is a
combination of vision, understanding, and program implementation
skills.*

Human Resources Development Leadership and the Creation of a Learning Organization

Manuel London

Human resources development (HRD) professionals are a source of expertise on organizational assessment and change. HRD interventions encourage continuous learning through improved performance management. This chapter explores the role of the HRD function in using these interventions to establish a continuous learning environment in work organizations. It shows how training and development contribute to new directions in management. These changes empower employees to recognize emerging organizational requirements and to work together to improve quality and meet customer expectations. Further, these changes require employees to assume responsibility for their own continuing education and career development in line with organizational expectations and opportunities.

The Changing Organizational Environment

Five to ten years ago, HRD was viewed as a support function in many organizations. Large corporations and government agencies had their own training departments to provide necessary technical courses. Often, the training departments were asked to run management development courses. These were basic courses in supervision and related management concepts, such as organizing work, time management, and conflict resolution. The curricula were based more on what was in vogue at the time or on the whims of top management than on the particular needs of the organization. Small organizations were less likely to have their own training departments and probably turned to outside vendors to run programs. Alternatively, employees were sent to university-run short courses. In these firms, training was viewed as a "nice to do" expense, but one that could be easily eliminated in tight economic times.

More recently, organizations have been undergoing major cultural transformations as they struggle to survive in an increasingly competitive, financially strapped world economy. Since the early 1980s, a revolutionary change has been unfolding in business, government, and nonprofit organizations. New technologies, from computer-integrated manufacturing systems to digital mobile communication networks, have changed the nature of many jobs. One response to these changes has been downsized organizational structures that increase managers' spans of control and require employees to do more with less. Another response has been the adoption of total quality management principles and techniques for continuous improvement of work processes.

Buzz words of the 1990s are *empowerment, teamwork, alliances, flexibility,* and *quality.* By-the-book bureaucratic management is out. Customer-responsive, development-oriented management is in. Employees are called *associates* and managers are called *coaches.* The coach's role is to support the continuous development of his or her associates so that they are better prepared for today and the future.

Toward Continuous Learning Organizations. In a recent issue of *Harvard Business Review,* Peter Drucker (1991, p. 78) wrote about the importance of continuous learning to productivity improvement: "Continuous learning must accompany productivity gains. Redesigning a job and then teaching the worker the new way to do it, which is what Taylor did and taught, cannot by itself sustain ongoing learning. Training is only the beginning of learning. Indeed, as the Japanese can teach us, . . . the greatest benefit of training comes not from learning something new but from doing better what we already do well."

Organizations that run by continuous learning are referred to as *adaptive companies* and *learning organizations.* Consider the example of Granite Rock, a unionized supplier of gravel, crushed stone, and other building materials in Watsonville, California ("Company Profile . . . ," 1992). The firm employs about four hundred people and does about $90 million of business a year. The company spends about $1,000 a year per employee on training. The weekly newsletter announces the "Graniterock University" training schedule. Courses are offered on such topics as statistical process control, plastering, hydraulic systems, and leadership. In-house seminars on company time broaden technical skills. Also, employees are encouraged to take advantage of tuition assistance for courses at the local college. Training is available to workers of all ranks. The firm's philosophy is simple: "Training obviously makes for smarter, more well-rounded employees. It provides another benefit, too: it undermines the us-against-them mentality characteristic of both employees and management in many union shops. White-collar and blue-collar workers attend the same sessions, hear the same ideas, live in the same lodgings when they travel. It's that much easier for them to see their problems as common" (1992, p. 66).

As Drucker (1991) suggests and the Granite Rock example emphasizes, continuous learning is essential to an increasing number of employees. The HRD function provides the guiding expertise. Organizations are experimenting with new ways of doing business. HRD is at the forefront of these changes by conceptualizing, communicating, and teaching new behaviors. The HRD function is helping to redefine the role of manager and executive as managers shift from being monitors and controllers to coaches and mentors. HRD is interpreting environmental changes, analyzing their implications, and generating learning programs that allow employees to adapt to these changes.

The imperative of continuous learning means that HRD becomes a central function in the organization, not just a support function. Organizational decisions cannot be made without considering HRD implications. For instance, the process of deciding where to locate a plant requires information about the skills available in the local labor force. The process of deciding to implement a new technology requires information about current employees' skills and their ability to learn. In some cases, HRD drives organizational decisions. For example, HRD analyses may point out learning gaps that must be corrected, or analyses may demonstrate special capabilities that allow the firm to develop new products and services or to enter new markets.

Leadership and HRD. Leaders of continuous learning organizations recognize that HRD is vital to their own success and the success of the enterprise. In these organizations, the HRD head can work in partnership with the organization's other officers to establish directions for development and then provide the learning mechanisms to make continuous learning a reality. The HRD vice president or director may be an integral part of the organization's top-management team. Also, the HRD director may have an advisory board of top managers who guide learning initiatives.

Development activities are not stand-alone efforts in continuous learning organizations. They are an integral part of people's jobs. They encompass individual learning and team development. They include all modes of learning, not just classroom training. Computer-based training, on-the-job training, job aids, videos, hot lines, and numerous other learning technologies and strategies are now available. Also, HRD must be integrated with other human resources functions to ensure a comprehensive approach to selecting, educating, evaluating, and rewarding people.

The scope of HRD is broadening to encompass the tasks of changing and reinforcing a firm's organizational culture. Training objectives include orientation of newcomers and teaching entry-level skills, retraining dislocated workers, improving group effectiveness, reinvigorating burned-out workers, ensuring maximum use of technology, and developing high-potential managers (Chmura, Henton, and Melville, 1987, p. 17).

Learning methods and curricula must be tied to the organization's goals and each employee's specific objectives. Also, they must have immediate payoff and long-term benefit to drive the current and future success of the enterprise. This means that HRD leaders must play a key role in establishing and implementing organizational strategies. This has become especially important in financially constrained, increasingly competitive environments. Downsizing organizations must ensure that the people who remain are prepared to meet current and future job requirements and high work demands.

Cases have been reported of organizations fostering continuous learning in downsizing organizations (London, 1987; London and Mone, 1987). Methods include professional development programs that outline organizational strategies, related managerial dimensions, and curricula. These programs may require career planning, and they may offer fast-track management development programs for high-potential managers. The programs are designed to reflect changing organizational strategies. For instance, flatter organizational structures lead to fewer people in the fast-track programs. Increased attention to customer-responsive management and empowerment of subordinates serve to foster and reward different management behaviors from what were once important.

HRD and Organizational Change: Building a Leadership Platform

The organizational changes described above have implications for the kind of leadership needed in organizations. Knowledge about requisite leadership and managerial skills can guide the types of people who are hired and promoted into management and the developmental experiences that are necessary to prepare people to meet changing job demands. Therefore, the conceptualization of leadership and management skill dimensions drives a variety of human resources functions, including selection and staffing, development, appraisal, and compensation.

One approach to establishing key leadership dimensions is to analyze the jobs and behaviors of successful executives. The results are contrasted with behaviors of average or less successful executives in order to identify key dimensions for success. Such job analyses should identify the dimensions of successful performance that, in turn, can be used to guide training and human resources systems (Kraut, Pedigo, McKenna, and Dunnette, 1989). This kind of analysis, when conducted periodically at different levels of the organization, provides the information needed for calibrating

HRD procedures, such as assessment centers, to ensure that they are tapping the right skills and giving managers feedback on fruitful behaviors. However, procedures such as these are focused on current behavioral requirements, not on what will be required and not on directions for change. This suggests the need for a prospective orientation, or what might be called *future-jobs analysis.*

Recognizing the changing nature of the business and the need to revamp human resources systems, one organization asked its officers to define their view of leadership requirements. The effort was led by the vice president in charge of HRD, with facilitation by experienced HRD managers. Outside experts were hired to talk about trends in business and management. During a series of meetings, the executives generated a set of leadership dimensions that became the hallmark for operating the business. The resulting dimensions included concepts such as motivating and energizing others, building and managing teams, interpersonal flexibility, developing people, valuing diversity, business knowledge and acumen, business results, and building information networks. Other dimensions focused on the increasingly competitive environment: applying leading-edge technology, understanding foreign cultures and markets, managing across organizational lines, taking charge of new or struggling projects, leading an organizational change, interfacing directly with customers, and leading a team of diverse people.

Each of these dimensions was defined so that all of the executives could agree on their meaning. Then they were used as the basis for personnel decisions and development programs. Called "the leadership platform," the dimensions were communicated to all employees in company newsletters. The chief executive officer (CEO) wrote a memo outlining the dimensions and explaining their importance to the organization's success. They were incorporated into criteria for the selection of managers. Also, they were used by departments with surplus managers to determine who should stay with the firm and who should be asked to leave. Assessment instruments were distributed to help managers evaluate their own strengths and weaknesses and talk with their bosses about developmental needs. Needs assessments evaluated skills of current managers in relation to the new skill requirements. A curriculum of management courses was designed to provide training in all of the areas. An upward feedback process was developed that asked subordinates to rate their supervisors on the dimensions. The feedback reports were given to managers to help guide their development. Performance appraisal forms were developed to include ratings on the dimensions, and the compensation system and promotion process were revamped to reward managers who demonstrated these skills.

The leadership dimensions were not meant to be static. Indeed, the next year, another series of executive meetings was held to revise the leadership platform. Different dimensions were emphasized and a few new ones were added. For instance, international sales became more important as foreign competitors entered the market and domestic sales decreased. As a result, emphasis was placed on learning about global competition and valuing cultural diversity. Experience in living and working abroad became essential to management development. Courses were offered to assist transferring managers in adapting to foreign cultures. Other courses explained business norms in different cultures. Another change reflected the increasingly diverse domestic labor market. More people with diverse ethnic backgrounds were hired to meet the firm's growing human resources requirements. Leadership dimensions highlighted the ability to lead heterogeneous work teams.

Integrated Performance Management Program. New ways of doing business require new human resources systems. Consider, for example, a firm that has downsized several times during the last few years. The surviving employees, while the cream of the crop, feel beleaguered. Their job demands have increased without a commensurate addition of resources. The employees are expected to make decisions to meet customer expectations. But they worry about their job security. Consequently, they avoid risks and try to understand and follow company policies and regulations. The firm wants to induce better communication between managers and their work teams. However, objectives are rarely set, performance reviews are perfunctory, and performance feedback is given only once a year during a formal review session, if it is given at all. Employees are categorized in a forced distribution that requires managers to rank-order group members, placing a prespecified percentage in each performance category, for instance, 10 percent in the lowest category, "fails to meet objectives"; and 10 percent in the highest category, "far exceeds expectations."

A change in this demoralizing organizational culture began when a new CEO was appointed. He was an entrepreneur who had experience at the helm of a fast-growing, high-technology firm. The new CEO challenged the HRD director to establish a human resources system that would improve communication, require objective setting in line with the organization's overall objectives (set by the CEO), establish a development plan for each employee in line with skill requirements to meet the individual's objectives, provide periodic performance feedback to employees, and eliminate forced choice and rating appraisal formats.

Called the Performance Excellence Program, the new system was built on elements of good management that were well known by the firm's managers but were not carried out or not done well. Focus groups were held to ask managers about barriers to better performance management and ways to facilitate better management in line with the CEO's performance goals. The resulting program consisted of the following components:

Setting of the Firm's Vision, Mission, Values, and Objectives. The CEO worked with the head of the HRD department and other officers to agree on a direction for the firm and expected behaviors. Values included honesty, integrity, concern for people, and valuing of diversity. Mission included enhancement of customer satisfaction through continuous quality improvement. The vision included increasing profitability, becoming the low-cost provider (the ability to be competitive and take advantage of flexible profit margins), and being the leader in technological advancements. The objectives were more specific to the firm's position in the market and the needs of current employees, for instance, acquisition of skills to implement specific technologies that were on the verge of implementation.

Methods to Communicate the CEO's Objectives for the Organization to All Employees. Communication methods included bulletins, videos, and group meetings. The goal was to have the objectives cascade down through the organization so that each individual's objectives would contribute to the overall organizational objectives.

Joint Objective-Setting Process. Supervisors and subordinates were expected to jointly establish annual performance objectives. These would be reviewed several times a year and adjustments made as priorities changed.

Establishment of Performance Measures. The objective-setting process required a determination of appropriate measures and targets for accomplishment. Some measures would be objective, such as the number of units sold, the number of on-time deliveries, and the number of defects. Other measures would be more subjective, such as customer satisfaction ratings. A distinction was made among measures that capture inputs, process, and outcomes. An example of an input measure is assurance that employees have the necessary knowledge and skills, perhaps as indexed by test scores or attendance at certain training programs. An example of a process measure is degree of contribution to team cooperation, possibly determined from co-workers ratings. Output measures would be a reflection of sales, product delivery, revenues, profits, or expenses. It was anticipated that all three types of measurements would be used.

Development Plan for Every Employee. Employees were expected to have a development plan that would list any experiences and training needed to accomplish each objective. Development objectives would also be based on skill requirements anticipated to do well on the job in the future, such as learning computer skills that would be needed for planned system changes. In addition, the development plan would include educational experiences to prepare for other jobs, possibly in other departments and at higher organizational levels. These career goals would be based on individual interests and information about the evolving needs of the business. Similar to objective setting, the task of establishing the development plan would be a joint process between the employee and the supervisor.

Quarterly Performance Reviews and Feedback. Supervisors were required to meet with subordinates every three months to review performance and revise objectives. More frequent feedback was encouraged as well.

End-of-Year Performance Evaluations. These would be narrative statements of accomplishment of each objective with measurements used as supporting material. Ratings and forced distributions would not be used. In this way, individuals were appraised against their own objectives, not in competition with each other. Resulting merit compensation would be based on the achievement of objectives, the difficulty of the objectives, and how the objectives were achieved, for instance, in a way that promoted cooperation and built alliances.

Orientation training was designed to communicate the new program. Courses were offered on the manager's role as coach and developer, including feedback skills and how to write constructive narrative performance reviews. Surveys and focus groups ensured that managers were following the new performance excellence program.

This program demonstrates the integration of HRD with organizational strategies and human resources tools, such as performance appraisal and compensation. As the objectives changed, new priorities were set and different behaviors emerged as keys to success.

Total Quality Management (TQM). TQM is another example of the strategic role of HRD in setting and accomplishing organizational objectives. Almost ubiquitous in business and government institutions, TQM principles and structures are a method for continuous improvement and satisfaction of customer expectations (see Tenner and DeToro, 1992, for an in-depth description of the process and content of TQM). Borrowing techniques from Japanese management, TQM relies on quality-improvement teams to establish improvement areas, collect data on customer expectations, examine barriers to productivity, and make changes. These tasks require that team members learn group dynamics skills. Team leader training teaches employees how to head quality-improvement teams. Other employees learn facilitation skills.

Training and facilitation are essential for introducing TQM. As employees are trained and participate in numerous quality-improvement teams, the ideas of continuous improvement and learning become ingrained in the organization. Ultimately, team management, identification of improvement areas, and use of team-building and group dynamics exercises and tools all become second nature. The result is a flexible organization that can form new group structures to respond to changing demands.

While HRD is necessary for a successful TQM program, TQM requires top-level commitment and initiative. The CEO and other top executives must show total commitment to TQM and must lead the effort. As such,

HRD becomes integral to the way leaders run the organization. HRD is not merely a support function or a linkage to organizational objectives. Rather, it is part of the organizational transformation.

Planning for Future Human Resources Needs. HRD leaders can encourage the organization's executives to think about future human resources requirements and what actions should be taken now to meet these requirements. The case of a medium-size firm (about seven hundred employees) with a new international business provides an example. The CEO and vice presidents of the corporation, including the HRD director, established a new business strategy that required input from a variety of sources, including considerable information about human resources. In particular, the HRD director provided information on the external and internal environments that helped the officers understand the human resources implications of their decisions.

First, the HRD department conducted a training gap analysis that compared employees' current training against the training that they should have to be effective. This research revealed areas where training was needed to bring employees up to par.

Second, the HRD staff created several alternative business scenarios. For example, they considered what would happen if the firm expanded in the southeastern United States and in Central and South America. They also considered what would happen if the firm remained mostly in the New York area and expanded sales in Europe. The scenarios outlined the types of personnel who would be employed by the firm and the cultural differences that would have to be prevalent and valued in the company's work force.

Third, using the scenarios and alternative directions in new technology, the HRD staff conducted a future-jobs analysis by interviewing officers and department heads about future job characteristics and skill requirements.

Fourth, the training gap analysis and the future-jobs analysis suggested the kind of training that employees needed to prepare for the future. The HRD director presented the officers with ways to provide this training and with the associated costs.

Fifth, the HRD director examined turnover trends in the organization and conducted a retirement eligibility analysis to indicate how many people would be likely to leave the firm during the next ten years. This had implications for selection and promotional opportunities.

Sixth, the HRD staff collected information about demographic trends and the external labor market in the regions where the corporation had offices and manufacturing facilities. Working with data from the U.S. Census Bureau and Department of Labor, the HRD director identified geographical areas that would have people with desired education levels. (Other officers investigated information about local economy, tax structures, and transportation, as well as other key information that would help make decisions about facilities expansion.)

Finally, once the new business strategy was decided, the HRD director and staff developed materials that communicated the strategy to employees. They described the implications of the strategy for skill development and how the organization would help people upgrade their skills. They wanted employees to understand the need for continued learning to meet new requirements. They also hoped employees would be enthused about emerging career opportunities as a result of the new business directions.

Leadership Roles for HRD Managers

The above examples suggest emerging leadership roles for HRD managers. Development is a responsibility shared by all employees. Employees take responsibility for their continued learning. Managers at all organizational levels take responsibility for their own development and the development of their people. In this sense, HRD is not limited to the training department. However, HRD experts are called on to define and direct employee development in line with organizational initiatives. This leadership function is prototypical of HRD management in successful organizations. Consequently, HRD administrators are challenged to develop leadership skills and behaviors. The following recommendations capture essential components of HRD leadership.

Become an Expert in Environmental and Management Trends. Executives will expect HRD managers to be experts in all facets of changing organizational environments. HRD managers need to comprehend shifting financial conditions and markets as well as demographic trends. Also, HRD managers will be expected to be on the cutting edge of management techniques that respond to these environmental changes. This can be accomplished by reading the latest periodicals and books, attending professional conferences, and participating in networks of training professionals.

Become Knowledgeable About the Operations of the Organization. HRD managers cannot be functional specialists who operate in an ivory tower independently of the day-to-day operations of the organization. The clients of HRD are other departments in the organization. An understanding of these clients' needs and expectations is necessary for HRD to be useful. The HRD director may establish an advisory board of fellow directors to ensure that training objectives help the organization accomplish its goals. Subject matter experts from other departments can be called on to help design training programs. An early warning system can be established to alert HRD managers to the emerging training needs in other departments as organizational and technological changes are contemplated.

Demonstrate the Value of HRD in Establishing Organizational Strategies. HRD managers should be viewed as partners by fellow executives and managers in establishing strategies and operational programs. However, the importance of this role for HRD will evolve as HRD managers prove their value to the success of the organization. Facilitation of the development of a leadership platform is one way to demonstrate this value and involve top executives in HRD initiatives. Human resources forecasting and planning is another.

Facilitate New Business Directions and Associated Leadership and Managerial Dimensions. HRD managers can be the impetus for new organizational cultures and associated behavioral changes. They can suggest the need for change, lead group discussions about strategies for change, and develop systems and programs to communicate, train, and reinforce employees for implementing culture change. The Performance Excellence Program described earlier is an example of such an effort.

Engender a Participatory Atmosphere for Establishing HRD Directions. Employees' commitment to HRD programs stems from their involvement in the planning of the effort. Also, involvement helps to ensure that the program meets the needs of the organization.

Work in Tandem with Other Human Resources Professionals to Develop Organizationally Responsive, Integrated Human Resources Systems. The examples in this chapter demonstrate the integration of HRD with other human resources functions. Training is not an isolated activity. The organization needs procedures that work together and are mutually supportive. This requires coordinated efforts and cooperative relationships among different HRD experts and functions.

Serve as Role Models of New Behavioral Styles. Organizational transformations require different behaviors in all departments of the organization, including the HRD department. Training experts should be role models for the programs that they develop and teach. For instance, they should apply TQM principles to better understand their clients' expectations and needs for cost-effective, responsive learning systems.

These leadership roles foster continuing attention to HRD in learning organizations. Leadership does not mean sole proprietorship of the HRD function. Also, it does not mean taking unilateral command. Rather it means sharing knowledge and encouraging participation in the development of new work processes and support systems. HRD professionals have an ongoing responsibility to highlight changing conditions, facilitate strategy formulation, and establish directions for employee and management development. As such, HRD professionals are change agents as well as educators.

In conclusion, HRD's role is pivotal to organizational success. The exciting and demanding challenge for HRD professionals is to apply the leadership roles to the HRD function. In this way, training professionals will be continuously alert to how HRD must adapt to meet changing organizational demands.

References

Chmura, T. J., Henton, D. C., and Melville, J. G. *Corporate Education and Training: Investing in a Competitive Future.* Report No. 753. Palo Alto, Calif.: SRI International, 1987.

"Company Profile: Granite Rock." *Inc. Magazine,* March 1992, pp. 58–70.

Drucker, P. "The New Productivity Challenge." *Harvard Business Review,* 1991, *69* (6), 69–79.

Kraut, A. I., Pedigo, P. R., McKenna, D. D., and Dunnette, M. D. "The Role of the Manager: What's Really Important in Different Management Jobs." *Academy of Management Executive,* 1989, *3* (4), 286–293.

London, M. "Employee Development in a Downsizing Environment." *Journal of Business and Psychology,* 1987, *2,* 60–72.

London, M., and Mone, E. M. *Career Management and Survival in the Workplace: Helping Employees Make Tough Career Decisions, Stay Motivated, and Reduce Career Stress.* San Francisco: Jossey-Bass, 1987.

Tenner, A. R., and DeToro, I. J. *Total Quality Management.* Reading, Mass.: Addison-Wesley, 1992.

MANUEL LONDON is professor in the Harriman School for Management and Policy at the State University of New York, Stony Brook.

Continuing professional education has evolved from a central focus on technical competence to a broader conception of reflective practice; in this context, the task of rethinking the roles of professionals in our society remains the principal challenge for leadership.

Active Learning in Continuing Professional Education: The Challenge of Leadership

James C. Novak

Traditional views of the goals of continuing professional education (CPE) have been questioned repeatedly in the literature of the last decade (Houle, 1980; Schön, 1983, 1987; Cervero, 1988). It would be inaccurate to claim that functionalism and technical rationality, which have served as our guides for so long, have been superseded. Nonetheless, the alternative approaches represented by reflective practice and critical theory have a logic and an appeal that are attractive to the entrepreneurs as well as the social activists in CPE. Alternatives have not yet been well operationalized in CPE settings, although case study research has been recommended as a way to build new notions of how to work with target groups (Brookfield, 1986; Merriam, 1988; Cervero, 1988). This chapter provides a description of choices in CPE planning and teaching that are available to educators. I believe it is feasible to blend functional and reflective goals in our program designs. Techniques of active learning in which the learner is encouraged to untangle problems and propose solutions (McKeachie, Pintrich, Lin, and Smith, 1986; Bonwell and Eison, 1991) can be employed for functionalist purposes and for reflection. An example from my experience in pharmacy continuing education is used to illustrate the leadership opportunities that emerge in attempting to help practitioners train for dramatically expanded professional tasks and work through the barriers to fulfillment of the new vision of the profession.

Leadership in Pharmacy

To "count, pour, lick, and stick" is a familiar refrain to pharmacists. Often, they use it to describe in a rueful and self-deprecatory way the prevailing public image of their main professional tasks. In an overly compact way, this doggerel summarizes the physical steps in dispensing medications. In the first half of the refrain, a drug (solid or liquid) is measured out into a container; in the rest, where assonance gives way to true rhyme, a label is affixed with the name of the patient, product, and physician, perhaps some general indication of when and how to take it, and possibly a word of caution about anticipated side effects.

The absurdity of this snippet of poetry is that five or six years or more of heavy coursework in the natural sciences, and any number of years of on-the-job experience, are reduced to routine and more or less trivial tasks, which could be performed, and in many settings are in fact performed, by much less extensively trained technicians, or by machines. On the other hand, pharmacists have a positive image as drug experts. No other health care professionals—physicians or nurses, for example—receive such extensive education in how drugs work: pathophysiology, pharmacology, pharmacokinetics, medical chemistry (Kessler and Rubin, 1992). Add to that background an access to a patient's medical history and status, such as that found in a hospital bedside chart, and an experienced pharmacist is well positioned to take an important role in drug therapy. In the hospital, some carry the label "clinical pharmacist" and visit patients, check charts, and consult with physicians and nurses.

Some pharmacists play additional roles as drug experts in the hospital. They participate with physicians in formally established administrative committees that have the power to choose which drugs will be routinely stocked, and to study how most effectively and inexpensively to use drugs.

Most pharmacists work behind a counter in a retail store, or community pharmacy. Whether in an independent store, a chain pharmacy, or the outpatient window at the hospital, pharmacists dispense the drug product to patients, and, as time and personal interest permit, they may have some opportunity to dispense drug information as well. This opportunity is diminished due to time pressures in the retail setting and especially to lack of access to medical records.

Pharmacy leaders are now discussing a larger role for pharmacists that would take them well beyond counseling patients about side effects and interactions, or encouraging patients to adhere to the proper schedules for taking their medications (Knowlton, 1991; Newton, 1991). Pharmacists are encouraged to assume greater responsibility for managing drug therapy, that is, monitoring progress, assisting in the choice or change of therapy, consulting with physicians, and collaborating with other health care providers. Pharmacists are thereby to become activists on behalf of the patient's overall quality of life, including medical outcomes (Hepler, 1991; Hepler and Strand, 1990; Wolf, 1991).

If they are to share responsibility and decision making for quality, results, and cost of therapy, they will need equal access to patient records, and they will need to receive input from physicians on demand. Here is where some of the barriers to the new roles become apparent.

These new aspects of the pharmacist's clinical role are clearly in the same arena as the physician's. The idea of pharmacists counseling patients already causes strains in the physician-patient relationship, as perceived by the physician, at least. Monitoring and codirecting of drug therapy will inevitably strain the pharmacist-physician relationship still further. Encouraging this perception are the pharmaceutical industries, which are unwilling to see their influence on prescribers diluted by additional interventions from pharmacists, the drug experts who can be very effective at countering their sales messages.

Advocates of increased pharmacist participation in drug therapy management have called it "revolutionary" (Wolf, 1991; Pew Health Professionals Commission, 1991) and "a paradigm shift" (Hepler, 1991). These advocates are seeking help from educators who might assist practitioners in the design and testing of training experiences that allow for the development of needed skills and elaborate the model of new practice.

Goals and Processes in Program Development

Historians have explored the theme that America is a culture of professionalism, and that higher education has served as a primary vehicle for individual aspirations toward achievement and self-realization (Bledstein, 1976). For the past one hundred years or so, when a person makes an occupational decision to pursue a professional or technical career of some kind, he or she is making a decision to become involved in higher education at some level. Today, higher education and jobs are linked extensively at both the preservice and in-service stages. Surveys of university-based providers indicate that we consider our number-one task to be retraining and upgrading the nation's work force. Continuing education has conveyed the ambitions of adults through a variety of delivery models, such as part-time and evening study, in-service, contracts, and independent study. Such innovation in modes of delivery is an important creative contribution that continuing educators have made in professional education.

The content of CPE programs can at times be the epitome of "what's new." Program development staff stay on top of emerging technical information and professional procedures and organize updates for practitioners. Because professionals tend to demand this information, CPE content is likely to be revised more frequently and in more detail than are the preservice curricula. In CPE, specialization and currency are the orders of the day. Together with the facilitating formats and scheduling, CPE workers deserve commendation for their contributions to professionals' achievements and capabilities. When professional school deans and college presidents talk up their institution's lifelong commitments to their graduates, this effort of CPE workers is the sort of thing they usually mean. However, these accomplishments are essentially quite conservative and mimic the educationally least progressive aspects of preservice programs.

CPE programs are conservative to the extent that they focus on the same teaching materials—texts, articles, assignments, and tests—as are found in the regular, full-time curriculum for pregraduates. They are nonprogressive to the degree that the teaching techniques emphasize lecturing by the teachers and passive attendance by the learners, with little focus on the learners' own experiences and their problematic situations as professionals. Programming of this kind views professional life as an accumulation of information, and professional practice as a set of problems for which one has learned given techniques for producing workable answers.

Adult educators can interact with a target audience of professionals in innovative and progressive ways when they (1) help the audience appreciate reflective practice and distinguish it from a functionalist approach to the goal of technical competence; (2) encourage and construct situations of active learning, using the practitioners' work settings as contexts for teaching and learning, for applying knowledge, and for experimenting and discovering knowledge; and (3) focus attention on new or emerging visions of the target profession's role and assist its leaders in developing the new conceptions and its practitioners in achieving training experiences in those new roles. These three avenues to program development constitute opportunities for leadership in CPE. Each is described in the sections below.

From Technical Competence to Reflective Practice. Schön's (1983, 1987) studies of reflective practice have focused attention on how skillful professionals perform and how they think about what they do (Cervero, 1988). Schön is especially interested in how professionals use their knowledge to address problems that are typically viewed as so complex that practitioners have no solutions in their profession's repertoire. This question suggests an approach to teaching and learning that is highly interactive, problem based, and performance oriented, in a manner reminiscent of progressive education and the current discussion of critical thinking (Dewey, 1924; Meyers, 1986). Approximately twenty medical schools have embarked on curriculum experiments with problem-based learning (Kabat, 1991; Philip and Camp, 1990; Schmidt, 1989). The general approach is not likely to be completely foreign to practicing professionals; almost everyone understands the case-based or problem-based approach of discovering knowledge for oneself while solving practical problems, even if they have not had much personal experience with it.

Schön's work helps us distinguish three levels of knowledge that can be arranged hierarchically. The first is knowledge of facts or *knowledge that;* the second is *knowledge how,* that is, procedural knowledge or knowledge gained from experience; the third is *reflection,* which in this context refers to knowledge acquired when applying one's factual knowledge and procedural knowledge to a complex new problem. Technical competence in a field of health care practice includes procedural knowledge and is an important, essential, and rather difficult step up from simply possessing the technical information of a profession. Indeed, practice in selected problems is built into the training that professionals receive; research-based theory and technique are taught together, using well-formulated problems. Schön opposes this standard of training for technical competence, which assumes that practitioners solve problems simply by selecting the right technical means for a given situation. This kind of view of the professional's training overlooks the important real-life confusing problems of the day, which have no known solutions.

In recent years, the general public has become well aware that even the most elegant theories and seemingly powerful techniques can be empty and sometimes inimical to real progress on pressing social problems (Wald, 1991). From the practicing professional's point of view, such problems are outside the prepared store of solutions or solution strategies. The problems may be poorly constructed, compared to the classroom examples, and contain unique characteristics (including value conflicts) that make the selection of technical means a highly uncertain task. Thus, there is public frustration with the professions, probably intensified by the expectations for expert performance that the professionals (and their teachers) created.

Schön's work calls attention to the gray areas of practice, where straightforward applications of rigorous scientific knowledge are impossible, or irrelevant. His approach is to turn to those practitioners who do well in the most difficult types of professional practice. These unusually competent professionals exhibit a kind of practice that can be studied and emulated. The applied science, which they also know, is mediated by the arts of reflection: problem framing, implementation, and improvisation.

Schön uses the example of a civil engineer trained to build a road. How to build a road is the functionalist question. The critical approach asks what road to build, and also where and whether to build. This latter approach involves a good deal of interaction among professionals and clients; it is open to conflicts of values, efficiency issues, equity issues, and quality and cost issues.

In displaying technical competence in a typical drug store, or community pharmacy, the pharmacist handles a variety of professional tasks that are straightforward, right from the textbook, and solvable with clear, technical answers. For example, a pharmacist would take steps in a counseling session to try to ensure that a patient does not incur a serious reaction among his or her medications, which becomes a rather likely event when there are multiple drugs and multiple prescribing physicians, as is the case with some elderly patients. Many drug interactions are well established, technical facts (or probabilities), available as knowledge stored in the memory, in reference books, and even in computerized systems tied in with the cash register.

Professional expertise, or what Schön (1987, p. 22) calls "artistry," is displayed by the pharmacist working outside the reaches of usual textbook-type problems. With adverse drug reactions, the artist exemplifies competence at interviewing, identifying problems, and counseling. At each stage, the skills are multiple, and the employment of those skills a multitrack exercise of the many options available to the expert as he or she navigates through the uncertainties and complexities of a real patient's case.

In CPE for pharmacists, problem-based learning and reflection are rare. Didactic, lecture-based instruction predominates, despite the concern that mere transmission of the information does not bring competence, and that clinical practice is replete with complications, such as patients whose situations do not fit the predictions in textbooks.

Many pharmacy educators have pondered how to train undergraduates to be able to understand and then demonstrate these complex skills of problem solving and patient analysis in the clinical setting. Younger students progress in school almost exclusively on the basis of their abilities to learn and retain textbook-type information about given disease states and chemical entities. Consolidation of this information in the service of solving simulated cases in the classroom, or real cases in the clinic, presents a dilemma in teaching and learning. There is more or less no end to the technical facts that could be memorized for later use; and yet the ability to use facts in case applications is appallingly limited when students begin to try. Much more would be given to case problems if time were available in the curriculum. Along with time, there is also the issue of how to teach in order to build problem-solving skills. The usual device is to set aside time for case discussion but to continue the very heavy reliance on lecturing. This seems an unsatisfying way to provide programs aimed at developing clinical skills.

Active Learning in Program Design. There is a strong consensus among instructional psychologists nationally about active learning (Bonwell and Eison, 1991; Loacker, Cromwell, and O'Brien, 1986). Knowledge of facts, principles, and theories must be organized and elaborated by the learner in order to be retained longer than a semester and to remain available for use in new and different contexts. Some of the basic strategies to promote elaboration and organization include generating questions and synthesizing answers.

A more complex version of these tasks is participation in the design, conduct, and evaluation of a research project. "Researching" of a real patient's unique constellation of symptoms and history constitutes a similar task. In my view, reflective practice and the critical approach to professional work are in tune with the current emphasis on active learning at the collegiate level.

A related aspect of active learning is motivation. Learning situations that involve active learning seem to have the potential to build intrinsic motivation, the desire to continue to learn, self-confidence about learning, and the likelihood to apply knowledge in changed circumstances. Adult learners have the opportunity to acquire particular knowledge that sticks, and general aspects of "skill and will" (as the instructional psychologists say) that help them become more effective learners overall (Pintrich, 1988).

Faculty may find special satisfaction in teaching of this kind. It will probably also be appropriate to work with them on teaching tips for active learning. (Part of this chapter is devoted to such faculty development issues.) Students, some faculty allege, are passive notetakers, alienated from the heart of learning, which is active personal discovery of knowledge, attitudes, and skills. Students need to be exposed to other types of experiences, such as case simulations, role playing, and conducting their own research inquiries. The faculty's goal is the development of such abilities as critical thinking and problem solving, not rote memorization of facts based on information transmitted orally by the teacher; but most faculty need some guidance and encouragement to achieve this goal. Attempts to broaden our approaches to CPE by including noninstructional modes of learning face a threat from the overwhelmingly dominant belief that formal learning via instruction is the only valid method.

What does this turmoil about pedagogy mean for those of us in CPE? In a way, it means we were right to pursue an antiestablishment tone in our teaching, stressing the active involvement of the learner and the important interface between the individual learner's goals and the material "out there" to be learned.

Reflective Practice, Active Learning, and Inquiry. Thus far, I have connected the CPE leadership role in working with target groups to the distinctive goals of reflective practice, and to active learning in program design in support of these goals. Next, these concepts are revisited in the context of envisioning new roles for professional practice. *Professionalization* and *reprofessionalization* are terms that highlight the tendency of vocations continually to undergo changes in their sense of mission, knowledge base, and collective identity (Houle, 1980; Holloway, Jewson, and Mason, 1986).

At the moment, these dynamic aspects of their professional life are very apparent to most pharmacists, although the changes might be invisible to the lay public. The opportunity to take new and expanded roles in health care, and to define a more authoritative clinical position in drug therapy management, clearly will alter what is relevant in the knowledge base. Collective identity and levels of personal satisfaction will also be altered.

Houle (1980) helps us picture how the dynamic nature of professions affects lifelong learning options. He specifies three overlapping modes of learning, each of which relates to professionalization: inquiry, performance, and instruction. Learning through inquiry is likely to occur when a professional is looking at the "big picture" of practice, that is, asking, "What is my professional role, and how does a given, uncertain, complex problem relate to my sense of professional mission?"

Learning through performance and learning through inquiry are interwoven with professional practice. Performance involves development of one's mastery of theoretical and applied knowledge and one's capacity to solve problems. Inquiry is a process of creating, rather than disseminating. What emerges from an inquiry is not known in advance; rather, it is a new synthesis, technique, policy, or strategy for taking an action. The predictability of didactic instruction severely limits the effectiveness of the process of inquiry. In the performance mode, one learns by drill and repetition or practice in everyday work situations with real cases; thinking about the uncertain aspects of a given situation in which one is involved may drive one to learn, for example, by actively searching a data base or library shelf for the information needed. Habitual use internalizes the idea or skill via practice.

Among the three overlapping modes of learning, Houle encouraged us to use performance and inquiry more frequently. Obviously, we concentrate on the instructional mode. We are used to it and can manage it rather well. Laudably, sometimes we base it on the learner's needs. We try to avoid a lockstep approach and use modules. Skillful teachers can simulate performance and inquiry; but with answers known in advance, it becomes obvious that the framework is didactic and instructional. Performance learning, using the teacher's and the learner's actual ongoing experiences via on-site mentoring, is also rare. Inquiry can be somewhat structured through outlines, statements of principles, discussions, seminars, and clinical encounters, but the end products cannot be predicted; when learning happens, it is frequently a by-product of efforts to establish or evaluate policy, come to consensus, or implement a plan. Finally, the evaluation process for inquiry is idiosyncratic and programmatic: Did the inquiry lead to results that "worked"? Inquiry is slippery because one usually has to try hard to figure out how to state the problematic situation (as well as to apply the results).

Houle's (1980) inquiry mode of learning is similar in many aspects to what Schön calls reflective practice (and what John Dewey called learning by doing). Schön emphasizes the level of professional practice that he calls artistry, and how it might be encouraged by a form of education he likens to coaching. Schön looks to the "deviant traditions" of education for practice, in the studio and conservatory, and specifies "learning by doing" and "initiation into the tradition" by master practitioners, which he labels "the artistry of good coaching" (1987, p. 22).

The activities of learning by doing and receiving the right kinds of coaching constitute the reflective practicum. These lead to competence in the indeterminate zones of professional practice, where things are messy and there are no answers "in the book."

The coach (or master teacher, studio master, clinical supervisor, and so on) heavily relies on interpersonal skills to facilitate a teaching-learning dialogue, which helps reflection-in-action go "right," and to overcome the intellectual predicaments and paradoxes and the interpersonal conflicts that are inherent to the situation. Schön's examples of coaches, from management consulting and other situations, are described through subtle applications of concepts from the group dynamics and counseling literature: defensiveness, control, openness, risk taking, and a win-lose mentality. In his reflective practice books, Schön (1983, 1987) emphasized the group dynamics material and gave it a prominent place in his descriptions of how the reflective practicum works.

As adult and continuing educators, some of us might respond to Schön primarily in terms of the group dynamics of coaching as a situation for teaching and learning. Those of us who have taught adults in interactive situations are well aware of the effects of interpersonal forces on the learning environment, and we appreciate Schön's willingness to explore this area in depth, and his expertise at negotiating the conundrum of nondirective directive behaviors, for example.

Some of us will respond to his conception of the artistry of the expert and the ideal practicing professional. Most of our programming is for neophytes, and for spoon-feeding the latest technical rationality into practitioners. There is a greater status allure and an intellectual excitement in being at the top rung of the training ladder, with experienced professionals who aspire to artistry.

The key insight from Houle (1980) is the notion of inquiry as an opportunity for program development in CPE. Houle's ideas about inquiry as a mode of learning have helped me to understand Schön's concept of reflection-in-action, and to apply the concept in programming. Houle and Schön have enriched my understanding of how professionals learn, particularly the pacesetters who welcome challenging and highly involving forms of learning. Programs of this type or level aim to further the range and power and responsibilities of the profession—and the professional— beyond the current norm generally accepted by society. My theme is that such programs provide an opportunity for CPE leadership and cast a new light on adult and continuing educators as colleagues and partners in furthering the roles of professionals.

The avenues for learning, therefore, are broader than didactic instruction. We also learn by performing. We also learn in an open-ended, loosely structured way when we inquire about situations that have no single or well-established answer; such situations include problem solving through a synthesis of a great deal of knowledge and experience, not merely an application of a single, given rule. These may be unique patient care or managerial situations, with outcomes in doubt, and no technical answers that fit the cases neatly. An example is a complicated patient case involving quality-of-life issues, cost issues, and therapy decision issues.

To move beyond instruction, we need to create an interest in vocational specialization with specific aspects of the inquiry mode of learning. It is important to understand that inquiry is not exclusively functional or reflective but rather both: It is a higher-order functionalism, related to the expansion of professional roles (and thereby reflective) and undertaken via principles of active learning. The idea of master professionals who are sensitive communicators and coaches not only is limited by the short supply but also actually presents an old-fashioned, instructor-oriented model of the teaching-learning process. Instead, I opt for relying more heavily on the dynamic of professionalization and seeking competence for new professional roles via active learning.

Case Description: A Program for Pharmacists

Cervero (1988) has noted the dominance of prescriptive writing about program design and has called for descriptions of actual planning frameworks, to supply what Brookfield (1986) calls practical theories of continuing education. The following narrative, then, is a form of case study in CPE.

Professionalization and Inquiry. In pharmacy education, the prevailing view of the professional is in the functionalist mode, based on assumptions of technical rationality. The typical method of teaching and learning is information transmission in the lecture format. To be sure, the later years of study and training involve patient contact and an approach that frequently employs the performance mode; but faculty dissatisfaction with how most students perform, and calls for curriculum change, reinforce the conclusion that the lecture format is due for increased scrutiny in the future. More opportunities for problem solving and independent work, and less passive attendance to lecturing, are key reform elements under discussion for the preprofessional curriculum (Pew Health Professions Commission, 1991; Wolf, 1991). In the past few years, the idea of new roles for pharmacists is frequently referred to as provision of "pharmaceutical care," in an analogy to medical care (Hepler, 1991; Hepler and Strand, 1990).

At the practice level, medicine and pharmacy each contain elements of response to escalating health care costs, which are due in no small part to failures and omissions traceable to the practitioner-patient interaction, rather than to the absolute costs of technical goods and services. In both fields, the new term frequently used for the interaction component is *cognitive services,* as opposed to the more familiar professional services such as writing prescriptions or dispensing drugs. Cognitive services include the activities of recording and interpreting a medical history, identifying problems, and providing individualized information and counseling. Control of costs is the external, social condition that will contribute greatly to new roles for pharmacists.

Pharmacy presents opportunities for Houle's (1980) inquiry. Clearly, it is an actively professionalizing occupation. The pharmacy project was built around a growing awareness of new roles, responsibilities, and sources of income for pharmacists. Pharmacists and educators have talked about new roles for about twenty years. The old role is the pharmacist as dispenser of drugs, accurately and safely preparing medications according to a physician's order. There is a legal sanction that specifies this role, and the economics of pharmacy is based on fees for the professional service of dispensing. Advocates of the new roles point to the benefits, ranging from safety to cost containment available to a given patient and to society when pharmacists do more than dispense drugs and offer bits of information. Of course, it might be assumed that pharmacist job satisfaction (and intrinsic motivation to continue to learn) will also be positively affected. Professional inquiry became programming here.

Functions of the New Leadership Role. My story begins with a small group of professionals who wanted to change the practices of their field. Such a change had been discussed for years in the abstract, or with particular vignettes and anecdotes about a new professional whose role and functions with clients would be greatly enlarged; also, there would be some sort of increased payment for these new services. But there was little actual practice of the new role, despite the apparently widespread need for the services.

These innovative professionals, who included university faculty, were leaders who were able to provide a model of what the new services were like, and how others could learn to perform them. This model had been pilot-tested by them in their own practices and those of a few colleagues.

They worked with an education specialist to translate the service model into an education program. Because the professionals knew in advance what they wanted to say about the model and how it worked, their initial outline was oriented toward an instructional mode of teaching and learning. As the education specialist, I pushed for a more performance-oriented approach.

Our goal was to train a small group (perhaps twenty-five) of practitioners for the new professional role related to patient contact. Prior knowledge and positive attitudes about the role were assumed. Several skilled behaviors were identified as essential to the role, and these were scheduled for significant emphasis in the project. Circumstances allowed for combining the formats of independent study, followed by a live workshop, and then on-site instructive feedback.

We used Houle, Schön, and education psychologists to guide us conceptually and provide a framework. We were comfortable with the lack of hard and fast rules for achieving specific cognitive and affective goals; at the same time, we were excited by the possibilities of accomplishing some of the subtler outcomes that we had in mind.

It was our contention that if we were to prepare students to handle difficult problems without predetermined answers, such as experienced in many real cases, we had to abandon a teaching-learning style that relied on passive absorption. We chose active learning. Students would read, write, discuss, and be engaged in solving problems.

Pharmacists who participated in the program would develop their skills in assisting therapeutically complex elderly patients to avoid serious problems associated with their medication schedules. The pharmacists would provide more comprehensive patient counseling and follow-up, compared to traditional services in the community drugstore setting. The model of service, in brief, involves an initial medication history and consultation, followed by monthly sessions by appointment to ensure that the patient is properly maintaining his or her medication therapy and making progress. By working with a health maintenance organization, we would have medical data usually unavailable to community pharmacists. Also, we established mechanisms for two-way communication, in writing, between participating physicians and pharmacists.

Pharmacists received a comprehensive training program in three phases: a self-study preparatory phase, with practice case exercises, readings, and a multiple-choice exam; a day-long workshop, for groups of eight to ten, involving lectures, role playing, case-based group discussion, and video-taped demonstrations; and on-site, instructive feedback for each pharmacist, with observation and coaching in skills such as interviewing, problem identification, and counseling.

The full, four-part hierarchical program evaluation recommended for continuing education in the health profession (Dixon, 1977; Coons and Hanson, 1986) is at present scheduled. We will evaluate behavioral change at the practice site, improvements in patient health, and changes in health care costs, along with immediate general satisfaction and short-term changes in knowledge, skills, and attitudes. There is potential here to have a significant influence on the future role of the community pharmacist.

Each of the complex patient case studies resembles one of Schön's messy unique problems not in the book, or one of Houle's improvisational inquiries. We have designed our learning program to give a variety of types of practice for these sorts of problems. We move into real patient cases, which are used as instructional opportunities in the ongoing interaction and feedback, when pharmacists are back on site.

Pharmacists chose the program because of its challenging nature, and because of the opportunities for professional growth. They might be on the leading edge of a related movement in pharmacy that envisions pharmacists being paid a fee as medication managers or consultants. One nearly universal complaint of community pharmacists is that they are rewarded by superiors for the number and speed of prescriptions filled, not for their clinical or information-oriented problem-solving skills. We wanted the pharmacists to think about and practice (eventually with their own patients) the following technical functions:

1. Information gathering: Techniques for learning were lectures, role playing, and group discussion. Other activities included use of a medication history form in preworkshop activities, whereby participants analyzed a completed form for a simulated patient, and practice at conducting a history-taking session on an acquaintance.
2. Problem identification: Lecture and small group discussion of cases. A variety of types of problems were used. All common reference books and resources were made available for case discussion and practice. Action plans were written, based on identified problems.
3. Communication with patients (and with physicians): Lectures, group discussion, and videotaped demonstrations were used to illustrate effective communication techniques. Specific counseling strategies were used in simulated patient-educator sessions. Also covered were techniques for patient monitoring, feedback, and reporting needed information to physicians.

At the outset of the workshop, at lunch, and at the conclusion, general considerations and logistics were discussed. These sessions reinforced and extended information supplied in the preworkshop readings and independent study packet. Postworkshop activities were previewed, including the planned on-site instructional feedback. We provided a complete time-line sequence for seeing patients and continuing contacts.

Teaching and Learning in the Pharmacy Program. I have referred to active learning as the key to understanding reflective practice and inquiry as elements of program design in CPE. In this section, I frame the pharmacy project using active learning concepts.

The program was a mix of the three learning modes (instruction, performance, and inquiry). In our program design for performance and for inquiry, Schön's insights on education for artistry were influential in understanding the faculty's role as coaches. Active learning provided a framework for a number of choices about how and what to teach.

In recent reports, such as Bonwell and Eison (1991), there is increased specificity in use of the term active learning. Students must engage in tasks such as analysis, synthesis, and evaluation, as well as thinking about their own thinking. Dewey's classic views of education still apply, including his observation that learning is "an active, personally conducted affair" (1924, p. 390). Making the reverse point, Whitehead said that ideas that are received without being utilized, tested, or thrown into new combinations will be "inert ideas" ([1929] 1967, p. 1).

Transfer, learning to learn, motivation to learn, expertise: these are the major topics of interest in instructional psychology today. As cited earlier, the popular descriptive heading is active learning. We needed to talk about these subjects repeatedly in the program design process. It is easy to fall back into the standard format of didactic lecturing and passive learners. The tasks of revisiting these concepts and encouraging discussion of how to apply them to the outcomes desired by the target group were essential elements of my role in the design process.

Transfer is regarded as the key problem of learning, demonstrated by using knowledge in a situation different from the one in which it was originally learned. Recall of the knowledge in identical circumstances is memorization and information transmission. Problem solving involves seeing sufficient similarities in content so that one can transfer knowledge to a new circumstance and apply it.

Learner control and involvement is a matter of deep information processing, as the instructional psychologists see it. Such deep processing "encodes" material in memory in ways that are more conducive to transfer. The more practice, use, elaboration, and reorganization by the learner, the more transfer is likely.

Learning objectives help learners select the "right" facts for retention in memory but do little to help them make connections to other material, or to synthesize the facts with what they already know. Furthermore, unlike the so-called higher-order tasks, objectives do nothing to help learners make applications of the facts in external situations.

What is known about the skills of learning to learn has clarified the limitations of the information transmission metaphor. Learning how to learn is a matter of strategic learning, or focusing on what's important in, for example, a text. One of the best ways to improve students' learning is to help them become more aware of their thinking processes, and to negotiate or monitor their encounter with a text, rather than take it as a given chunk of uniformly important material.

Intrinsic motivation to learn new skills, continue to learn, and achieve one's learning goals is related to the techniques of active learning. The practice of actively encountering the material, as with cases, projects, and so on, is associated with increases in motivation. Also, thinking about one's thinking, or being a strategic learner, is associated with active learning. I conclude this section with questions and answers from my experience in the pharmacy project.

When Is Discussion Better than Lecture? We chose to incorporate a great deal of discussion time in our day-long workshop. To do this successfully, the faculty developed new teaching materials, brought a variety of references and other resources into the classroom, ran the risks of non-participation and loss of control, struggled with their feelings about coverage of content, and certainly increased their preparation time and anxiety level. What evidence convinced them that this was the way to go?

Aside from their own positive experiences in the past, they appreciated the major review of the research literature on the college classroom by McKeachie, Pintrich, Lin, and Smith (1986), which includes a strong endorsement. Discussion is preferable to lecture if the objectives of the course are to promote long-term retention of information, motivate students toward further learning, allow students to apply information in new settings, or develop students' thinking skills. Achievement of such goals requires faculty who are knowledgeable about alternative techniques and strategies for encouraging discussion, such as questioning, case studies, simulation, peer teaching, and in-class writing.

So Why Use Lectures at All? Our faculty gave minilectures at various points throughout the day. (It may have been that the anxiety to cover certain content overwhelmed us at times.) The research on aids to lecturing has been aimed at situations where active learning techniques are difficult, such as in large classes. This work has divided cognitive processes into three categories: selection, internal connections, and external connections. Lectures are especially good at helping learners select which facts should be retained; behavioral objectives bolster this aspect of lecturing. To arrange a process into a sequence, to enumerate its parts, or to make a generalization: these are internal connections, or synthesis; with care, lecturers can accomplish these outcomes well. The third type of cognitive process is making external connections, or applications, relating to prior knowledge (for example through models or analogies) and thereby resulting in applications to new settings. Notwithstanding the findings about the superiority of discussion for retention, application, motivation, and development of thinking skills, the lecture remains available for selecting facts and focusing attention, and for some kinds of synthesis and application.

What Can We Do to Help Learners Learn to Think More Like Experts and Less Like Novices? Instructional psychologists have pursued the notion that knowledge comes in two general forms, and that experts, such as Schön's reflective practitioners, can be distinguished from novices in an extension of how these two forms of knowledge are described. Novices can relatively quickly master semantic information, or "knowledge that," and try to use it to address problems. Experts do not have superior formulas for solving problems. Instead, they improvise, with no fixed way of operating, guided by context, experience, or case knowledge.

The intermediate steps of acquiring such expertise seem to be facilitated by guided instruction, with assessment and feedback. Both Schön's coaching and the pharmacy project's instructive on-site feedback seem to fit the expert-novice model.

Which Thinking Skills Are Being Improved? The general skills of thinking and problem solving encompass the ability to form plans, track progress, evaluate solutions, and so on. These skills seem similar to those of Schön's professional, who reflects while in action as a professional. Doing things and thinking about what you are doing are central to the instructional psychologists and to Schön. We provided pharmacists with a number of open-ended guides to structure their process of identifying problems, forming and communicating plans, and so on. Schön (1987, p. 40) distinguishes three hierarchical levels of learning and thinking. The first is to recognize and apply standard rules. The next is to reason from general rules to problematic cases, in ways characteristic of the profession. Finally, given success at the previous levels, the third is to develop and test new forms of understanding and action when the familiar categories and ways of thinking fail. Awareness of one's thinking process is in itself a higher-order skill associated with problem solving.

How Are People Likely to Be Motivated Enough to Do These Sorts of Things? Motivation is highly related to achievement. Whether we intend to work with a few pacesetters of a profession or an entire sector of the nation's work force, motivation will be a key consideration. Several studies have documented sustained and enhanced motivation through project-based learning, that is, partly self-directed investigations of nontrivial problems. Learners who ask questions, make predictions, design plans, collect data, draw conclusions, communicate findings to others, ask new questions, and create artifacts (in writing or other media) are likely to be highly motivated. The pharmacy project seems well suited to this kind of learning. Other considerations are an absence of predetermined outcomes (which Schön would second) and a driving or ongoing question or concern (in our case, a real patient).

In cases where the problems are not authentic and are wholly orchestrated by the instructor, there is much less potential for engagement. Cognitive engagement, therefore, enhances motivation and improves competence in the thinking skills.

Will Active Learning "Work" in Noncredit CPE? Several things are at issue. The basic subject matter might be more familiar to practitioners than to students, which would make them better active learners. But by definition, novices have trouble figuring out the right conditions for applying their propositional knowledge. Also there is the matter of spaced practice. Schön's students, as degree seekers working over a semester of three or four months, had the advantage of repeated cycles of assessment and feedback, and different contexts for application. Credit does not seem to be the significant issue.

Is There a Low-Risk Situation to Start with? Try familiar subject matter, and a short duration of active learning. Faculty must prepare new materials for the situation, but there is no need to revamp a whole course. An episode of active learning in a given lecture hour is a way to try it out. A similar tactic is to insert a cycle of "instruction-performance-inquiry" into an upcoming program as it is developed and to provide the target group with a sense of the less frequently used modes of learning.

Conclusion

Houle (1980, pp. 30–31) described the evolving role of CPE work as follows: "A dynamic concept of professionalization offers educators both the opportunity and challenge to use active principles of learning to help achieve the basic aims of the groups with which they work. They become not merely reinforcers of the status quo, as they so often are now, but the colleagues of all who work to further the power and responsibility of the vocation. They serve but are not subservient." It is clear that the traditional view of program design looks at needs assessment as an avenue to mass marketing and mass production of a standardized package delivered in the teacher-centered instructional mode, and that the new view puts far greater emphasis on decentralized student activities and individual student goals, but with no less openness to or capacity for a large number of learners.

Drug therapy, the most common form of medical intervention, is sufficiently inappropriate, ineffective, or harmful to place enormous personal and economic burdens on our society each year (Wolf, 1991; Hepler and Strand, 1990). Pharmacy leaders are calling on pharmacists to prepare themselves to assume a level of responsibility equal to that of physicians in managing the drug therapy of "their" patients. Shared decision making and accountability go well beyond dispensing of products, provision of routine drug information, or a minute of counseling beside the cash register. There are structural, logistical, and personal barriers: access to patient medical data, a payment mechanism for the pharmacist's time and services, training and assessing to ensure that current practitioners are capable of these responsibilities, and potential interprofessional antagonisms at the "medicine-pharmacy interface" (Campbell, 1989, p. 405).

In our pharmacy project, the instructional program was designed to stimulate knowledge, skills, and awareness appropriate to the new professional role. By using principles of active learning, we encouraged learners not only to become more competent but also to become more able to reflect on how they solve problems as professionals and deal with the complexities of individual patients. We used classroom simulations and on-site feedback as mechanisms to develop the ability to "do" and to "think about what one is doing." Our project provided multiple opportunities to gather and organize data, identify and analyze problems, and collaborate on solutions and on follow-up monitoring with other health care providers, particularly the patient's physician.

The CPE leadership challenge and opportunity is to guide the program design process away from an overemphasis on functionalism or technical solutions and toward reflective practice, which focuses on dealing effectively with situations that have no straightforward, textbook answers. Judicious advocation of the use of active techniques of learning will support the functionalist as well as the reflective goals. Compared to traditional ideas of the tasks of program design, I am less interested in needs assessment and more interested in instructional design. My interaction with the representatives of the target group is not as a vendor of packaged education products but rather as a partner in the development of materials and methods. By focusing on the new professional roles and services, we are productively involved in raising standards, as well as in raising revenue.

Perhaps we can market inquiry learning and learning for reflective practice. We can tout the attractive characteristics of expert performance and link them to inquiry. After all, we appreciate that adult learners in CPE want to believe, like Robert Frost's (1963, p. 171) woodcutter, that "work is play for mortal stakes."

References

Bledstein, B. *The Culture of Professionalism*. New York: Norton, 1976.

Bonwell, C. C., and Eison, J. A. *Active Learning:* ASHE-ERIC Higher Education Reports, no. 1. Washington, D.C.: George Washington University, 1991.

Brookfield, S. *Understanding and Facilitating Adult Learning: A Comprehensive Analysis of Principles and Effective Practices*. San Francisco: Jossey-Bass, 1986.

Campbell, W. H. "The Medicine/Pharmacy Interface." *American Journal of Pharmaceutical Education*, 1989, 53 (4), 404–407.

Cervero, R. M. *Effective Continuing Education for Professionals*. San Francisco: Jossey-Bass, 1988.

Coons, S. J., and Hanson, A. L. "The Need for Evaluation of the Ultimate Impact of Continuing Pharmaceutical Education." *Mobius*, 1986, 6 (4), 33–37.

Dewey, J. *Democracy and Education*. New York: Macmillan, 1924.

Dixon, J. K. "Methodological Considerations in Evaluating Continuing Education in the Health Professions." Paper presented at the annual meeting of the American Educational Research Association, New York, April 1977.

Frost, R. "Two Tramps in Mudtime (1934)." In *Selected Poems of Robert Frost*. Troy, Mo.: Holt, Rinehart & Winston, 1963.

Hepler, C. D. "The Pharmacist's Job Is to Provide Total Pharmaceutical Care." *US Pharmacist,* 1991, *16* (11), 61–68.

Hepler, C. D., and Strand, L. S. "Opportunities and Responsibilities in Pharmaceutical Care." *American Journal of Hospital Pharmacy,* 1990, *47,* 533–543.

Holloway, S.W.F., Jewson, N. D., and Mason, D. J. "Reprofessionalization or Occupational Imperialism?" *Social Science and Medicine,* 1986, *26* (3), 323–332.

Houle, C. O. *Continuing Learning in the Professions.* San Francisco: Jossey-Bass, 1980.

Kabat, H. G. *Problem-Based Learning: An Approach to Pharmaceutical Education.* Albuquerque: College of Pharmacy, University of New Mexico, 1991.

Kessler, D., and Rubin, I. "FDA Chief Answers Ten Questions on R Phs' Expanding Health Role." *Wellcome Trends in Pharmacy,* 1992, *14* (3), 3–7.

Knowlton, C. H. "Facts Transmission to Reflective Action." *American Journal of Pharmaceutical Education,* 1991, *55* (4), 365–369.

Loacker, G., Cromwell, L., and O'Brien, K. "Assessment in Higher Education." In C. Adelman (ed.), *Assessment in American Higher Education.* Washington, D.C.: Government Printing Office, 1986.

McKeachie, W. J., Pintrich, P. R., Lin, Y. G., and Smith, D.A.F. *Teaching and Learning in the College Classroom: A Review of the Research Literature.* Ann Arbor: National Center for Research to Improve Postsecondary Teaching and Learning, University of Michigan, 1986.

Merriam, S. B. *Case Study Research in Education: A Qualitative Approach.* San Francisco: Jossey-Bass, 1988.

Meyers, C. *Teaching Students to Think Critically: A Guide for Faculty in All Disciplines.* San Francisco: Jossey-Bass, 1986.

Newton, G. D. "Pharmaceutical Education and the Translation of Pharmaceutical Care into Practice." *American Journal of Pharmaceutical Education,* 1991, *55* (4), 339–344.

Pew Health Professions Commission. *Healthy America: Practitioners for 2005.* Durham, N.C.: Pew Health Professions Commission, 1991.

Philip, J. R., and Camp, M. G. "The Problem-Based Curriculum at Bowman Gray School of Medicine." *Academic Medicine,* 1990, *65* (6), 363–364.

Pintrich, P. R. "A Process-Oriented View of Student Motivation and Cognition." In J. S. Stark and L. A. Mets (eds.), *Improving Teaching and Learning Through Research.* New Directions for Institutional Research, no. 57. San Francisco: Jossey-Bass, 1988.

Schmidt, H. G. (ed.). *New Directions for Medical Education: Problem-Based Learning and Community-Oriented Medical Education.* New York: Springer-Verlag, 1989.

Schön, D. A. *The Reflective Practitioner: How Professionals Think in Action.* New York: Basic Books, 1983.

Schön, D. A. *Educating the Reflective Practitioner: Toward a New Design for Teaching and Learning in the Professions.* San Francisco: Jossey-Bass, 1987.

Wald, M. L. "As Science Gauges Perils in Life, to Learn More Is to Know Less." *New York Times,* Aug. 19, 1991, p. A1.

Whitehead, A. N. *The Aims of Education and Other Essays.* New York: Free Press, 1967. (Originally published 1929.)

Wolf, H. H. "Commission to Implement Change in Pharmaceutical Change: A Position Paper." *AACP News Special Report,* November 1991.

JAMES C. NOVAK is director of the Office of Educational Programs, College of Pharmacy, University of Michigan, Ann Arbor.

The evolving literature on leadership shows how our ways of thinking about this quality have changed. An understanding of how this research has been conceptualized can assist us in framing and pursuing our own learning projects on leadership.

Visions of Leadership: Understanding the Research Literature

Amy D. Rose

This chapter presents an analysis of some of the major views and trends in leadership research. The central questions of the research are the following: What are the qualities of leaders? How can we identify these qualities? And how can we foster them in promising individuals?

Although notions of leadership and industrial growth have been linked throughout the century, in the 1980s, leadership became the new buzzword for dealing with an assortment of social, political, and economic problems in the United States. Faced with perceptions of American decline and decay in manufacturing, industry, and education, writers championed a movement calling for a return to "excellence." This excellence involved a restoration of regard for the customer and an emphasis on innovation that could only be achieved through leadership. The concern here was the lack of leadership in American industry. By this account, leaders needed to go beyond the narrow constraints of the systems approach to management and to develop flexibility (Gardner, 1961; Gardner, 1990).

Thus, leadership lies at the core of administration and management, involving many aspects of good administration but going beyond these to include "vision" about the future. Whereas, previously, researchers wrote of managers and administrators, they now emphasized the role of the leader as an expanded manager who is also an "enabler" whose principal task is to "empower" subordinates, to give them latitude to innovate while motivating them and cheering them on (Bennis and Nanus, 1985).

Adult and continuing educators have adapted this concern with leadership and vision to their own needs and priorities. The primary emphasis

NEW DIRECTIONS FOR ADULT AND CONTINUING EDUCATION, no. 56, Winter 1992 © Jossey-Bass Publishers

is thus on the changing views of leadership and their implications for the practice of adult and continuing education.

Leadership as a Set of Individual Traits

In the first half of the twentieth century, researchers tried to identify and categorize the common or universal traits exhibited by leaders. As posed in psychological terms, the central precept informing this research was that leaders were born, not made, and that the task of the researcher was to identify leaders and then isolate the traits that made them tick. It was thought that if the specific, defining attributes of leadership were understood, then they could be identified in others and nurtured. Much of this research and study focused on what made great *men* great.

The study of traits varied greatly in orientation over the first part of the twentieth century. Everything from physical attributes such as height, weight, and physique to family background were studied in order to develop a model of leadership. But the results were typically impressionistic descriptions. Writers found that leaders had such traits as self-control, assiduity, common sense, judgment, sense of justice, enthusiasm, perseverance, tact, courage, faith, loyalty, flexibility, imagination, foresight, and versatility (Gouldner, 1950). One of the most noteworthy findings was the striking lack of correlation between intelligence and leadership (Fiedler, 1986).

The study of individual traits approached the question of leadership in terms of exceptional human beings. This effort, according to Gouldner (1950), divorced the leaders and their characteristics from the groups that they were leading, instead focusing on generalizable traits that, if only identified, would hold true in all situations. Several problems arose from these studies. First, the sheer number of possible traits was overwhelming. In addition, these were not usually prioritized or necessarily even distinct. The researchers also tended to blur the different uses of leadership and did not discriminate between the traits necessary for the ascent to leadership and those necessary for its maintenance. Most important, these traits were thought to be uniformly connected to specific behaviors and thus the behaviors were analyzed independently of particular contexts and situations. Finally, this approach, by simply listing personality traits, ignored the more complex, interactive aspects of personality. That is, there was a failure to recognize that the same trait could function differently in different people, resulting in different behaviors and different results (Gouldner, 1950; Bass, 1990).

One particularly influential branch of this trait analysis of leadership explored the idea of charismatic leaders. Indeed, much of the contemporary writing on leadership and its vision is a reworking of this earlier line of thought. The theological meaning of the term *charisma,* "a gift of God's grace that enables a human being to perform exceptional tasks," was adapted by Max Weber for sociological analysis, transformed from divine gift to a "gift of extraordinariness" bestowed by colleagues within an organization (Lepsius, 1986, p. 52; Bass, 1990, p. 185).

Since Weber, different definitions of charisma (much like the term leadership) have been debated. Weber's definition included five components of charismatic leadership, all of which are needed to constitute the category: (1) a person with extraordinary gifts, (2) a crisis, (3) a radical solution to the crisis, (4) subordinates or followers who are attracted to the charismatic leader because this leader connects them to "transcendent powers," and (5) validation of the phenomenon through repetition (Bass, 1990, p. 185). Thus, charismatic leaders inspired organizations, which, once established, became routinized or bureaucratized. Indeed, a basic aspects of the Weberian view was that once basic principles were formulated, managers and bureaucrats would take over. Thus, in this view, leadership is the basis of formation, not maintenance.

Since the 1970s, several empirical studies have tried to identify specific personality characteristics of charismatic leaders. Emotional expressiveness, referring to the use of nonverbal cues to motivate individuals to action, was often related to dramatic flair and included the propensity to maintain direct eye contact and exude a "magnetic attraction." In general, on personality inventories, females scored higher in emotional expressiveness and tended to be seen as more charismatic than males (Bass, 1990, p. 190). Another purported characteristic of the charismatic leader was self-confidence. These leaders were able to insist on the aptness of their positions because of their extreme self-confidence. They were unlikely to share feelings of discouragement with the public and would instead present themselves as the deliverers who could save a situation when everyone else had failed. Such leaders appeared to possess autonomy and lacked internal conflict. They were so convinced of the correctness of their positions that they were rarely conflicted over the rightness of their causes. Thus, they could easily reprimand subordinates and replace them if necessary (Bass, 1990). Such leaders also exhibited self-determination, that is, the characteristic that they and only they were in charge of their lives and their decisions. Such leaders were wedded to their ideals and presented themselves as outside of normal political life. But this same quality could also seem close-minded, dogmatic, and rigid and could indicate a mindset where differences of opinion were viewed as heretical rather than valid. Although most of the writing on charismatic leadership has focused on leaders of cults, religions, or societies, charisma resurfaced in the literature of the 1980s as an important component of transformational leadership.

Leadership as a Set of Behaviors

In the second half of the twentieth century, researchers found that because the number of traits was infinite, a more fruitful approach was to analyze the behaviors of leaders. Thus, leadership was not solely a psychological function but was also observable. Research then focused on leadership styles and the appropriate contexts for particular styles. An outgrowth of this research has been the construction of different leadership models that characterize the development of the individual leader within a particular organizational context. This meant looking at the individuals and the situations in which they were immersed. Leadership came to be seen as a relationship between people rather than as an individual trait and, as such, it could be learned. This new approach had important implications for the idea of leadership development, because unlike the earlier research emphasis on nurturance of innate qualities, the new contextual view afforded the possibility that anyone could learn the skills necessary to be a leader.

This aspect of the study of leadership built on Kurt Lewin's field theory. According to Lewin (1951, p. 45), field theory is not a theory but rather a methodology for "analyzing causal relations and . . . building scientific constructs." Lewin's purpose was to analyze sets of behaviors in particular fields in terms of the multiplicity of interacting factors making up the field. These sets included individual needs of the actor, how the individual views his or her actions, the groups to which the individual belongs, and all permutations of these relationships. All relationships are marked by a high level of interdependence, where changes in one individual change the other. Within organizations, this model of interpersonal relationships is somewhat different in that one individual can bring about changes in another without necessarily changing oneself. This is a power field. Power is the "capacity to exert influence" (Graumann, 1986, p. 87). Thus, power is not necessarily intentional; it is, rather, a potential act. Lewin's construct of power is an important aspect of his notion of leadership. For Lewin, leadership was a construct involving all aspects of group dynamics in terms of the distribution of the power field. Studies of the differences of power have led to the various characterizations of leadership from autocratic to participatory.

Although the study of leadership traits and power relationships focused initially on leaders in many contexts, but particularly in social, religious, and political milieus, the study of leadership as behavior has concentrated on leadership within organizations, particularly within business and industry. Much of the early work in this area simply listed the various functions of leaders. Thus, in 1940, Chester Barnard (1962) identified the functions of organizational leadership as the determination of objectives, the manipulation of means, the instrumentality of action, and the stimulation of coordinated action.

Very often, this functional approach mitigated the effects of the individual in order to focus on the situation. Yet, the most influential theories of leadership in the United States have been the more humanistic approaches that stress the development of individuals within organizations (Bass, 1990). Theorists from this school of thought range from Maslow, McGregor, Argyris, Likert, Blake and Mouton, and Hersey and Blanchard. For instance, McGregor (1966) developed his models of organizational leadership by comparing Theory X and Theory Y. Theory X assumed that workers were passive and needed to be tightly controlled. They needed to be motivated to work for organizational goals. In Theory Y, the leader assumed that subordinates were motivated and responsible and that the leadership role was to manipulate the environment so that it would be the most conducive for the achievement of individual and organizational goals.

Blake and Mouton (1964) developed a leadership grid that matched concern with people to concern with productivity. According to this theory, leaders who are high on both axes cultivate subordinates who are committed to the organization, who feel trust and respect for their superior, and who are also able to work in an interdependent fashion.

Models such as McGregor's Theory X and Theory Y and Blake and Mouton's managerial grid are attempts to address the complexity of the leadership issue. But they basically deal with leadership in terms of productivity, that is, how different leadership styles can affect (and, ultimately, increase) production. These models also move the notion of leadership beyond a discussion of traits or even of behaviors to a more complex view of the transactional nature of leadership.

Leadership as a Transaction

In earnest in the 1970s, researchers focused more closely on the nature of the interaction between the leader and the follower, seeing leadership as a dynamic process. Reaching back to Lewin's work, writers during this period examined interactions among individuals within specific situations. Studies were done on role conflicts, perceptions of role and function, the discretionary activities of leaders, and, most interesting, substitutes for leadership, which are structures or variables that either obstruct leadership or make it unnecessary (for example, bureaucratic organizations; Bass, 1990).

The most influential model of this era was Fred Fiedler's contingency theory, which dominated research through the 1970s. According to Fiedler (1967), the effectiveness of a leader is contingent on the situation. Thus, in certain situations a task-oriented leader may be most effective, whereas in others, the relations-oriented leader may be preferable. For Fiedler, the primary issue was how to place leaders or managers in situations where they would be most effective.

Other theorists looked more closely at the exact nature of the interaction between leaders and followers. These studies revealed that the effectiveness of leadership goes far beyond simple productivity. For example, Graen studied how leaders treat followers differently depending on individual situations. This evidence of context-sensitive leadership contradicts much of the earlier research, which tried to identify a uniform leadership style. Graen showed that the styles change within individuals (Bass, 1990).

Leadership and Organizational Culture

An important aspect of situational analysis is the examination of the organizational culture within which leadership is exercised. For example, Schein (1991) is concerned with examining leadership within a larger context. Thus, leadership is intertwined with culture formation, evolution, transformation, and destruction. When a particular culture becomes dysfunctional, leadership is needed to help the group or organization unlearn its cultural assumptions and adopt new ones. Schein's underlying premise is that organizations are created by human beings who also create their own culture through the articulation of their own assumptions. For Schein, the chief function of leadership is "the manipulation of culture" (p. 317).

Accordingly, leadership has different attributes depending on the point of development of an organization. For example, in the new organization, leadership must be able to embed its own assumptions so that they become part of the newly formed mission, goals, structures, and working procedures. An existing, functioning organization has different leadership needs at midlife. At issue is not the implantation of an organizational culture but rather the prevention of stifling cultural growth. Finally, within mature organizations, leaders may need to work to change the embedded culture.

Transformational Leadership

In the 1980s, an alternative paradigm of leadership took hold that focused on transformational leadership. The transformational leader asks followers to go beyond their own self-interests for the common good. Writers on this topic emphasize the importance of vision and the ability to communicate this vision and simultaneously enthuse followers to make it a reality. This view challenges the earlier emphasis on the hierarchical nature of organizations and the innate power of position within an institution. While these two factors are not written out of the equation, in essence the transformational approach shifts interest back to the individual and the development of individual leadership qualities.

This notion of transformational leadership owes much to the studies of charismatic leadership and the closely related inspirational leadership. In fact, according to Bass (1990), the two types of leadership cannot really be separated. But transformational leadership goes beyond charisma because it can be learned (Bennis, 1991).

When Burns (1978) first introduced the idea of the transformational leader, he viewed it as the opposite of the transactional leader. That is, Burns felt that true leadership went beyond contingencies and situational analysis. The literature on this view of leadership merges the components of previous research emphases. Thus, in terms of behavior, the transformational leader is able to set challenging objectives, provide meaning for actions, use symbols and images to convey ideas, manage impressions others have of these ideas, manipulate information, and build an organizational image (Bass, 1990; Bennis, 1991; Gardner, 1990).

Finally, in modern parlance, the transformational leader is enabling and empowering. This type of leader is able to envision a future state and then empower subordinates to work to achieve it. This skill involves both rational and emotional elements, such as inquisitiveness, the ability to plan, intuition, imagination, and insight. Finally, such an approach involves an aspect of consciousness-raising in that the leader must be able to help subordinates see old problems in a new light and therefore see the possibilities for innovation and change (Bass, 1990; Bennis, 1991; Schein, 1991).

This view of transformational leadership merges the old with the new. While paying lipservice to the idea that these skills can be learned, writers still emphasize the extraordinary individual. The question of how to teach someone to possess vision remains unanswered. There is much talk of vision, but little understanding about how to foster it. Certainly, attempts to develop vision within an organization with definite goals are quite different from similar efforts within a field, without an organizational structure.

Gender and Cultural Differences in Leadership

Current work on women and minorities as leaders warrants mention. It was first thought by feminists that women in leadership positions would bring a new style of leadership. They would be more relational and collegial, as well as better listeners, and would ultimately change the face of corporate America. At this point, the data are decidedly mixed. Some research indicates that women manifest different managerial styles from those of men, but, taken as a whole, no clear pattern of differences emerges. Other research suggests that women have different communication skills, tend to be more personal, and differ in their reactions to conflict and in their uses of power. But the evidence is not consistent and more work needs to be done in these areas (Astin and Leland, 1991). It is clear, however, that while their behaviors may not be distinctly different, men and women are judged differently by subordinates (Morrison, White, and Van Velsor, 1987).

One of the problems with this kind of research on gender differences has been the narrow constraints imposed on women's leadership. The questions are framed only in terms of traits and situations of women in formal, leadership positions. Since women are (or have been) excluded from these positions, the research has tended to find (in a good example of circular thinking) that women do not have the requisite traits. Astin and Leland (1991) tried to get around this problem by focusing on the leadership that women have exhibited in bringing social change, whether in formal roles or not. They reconceptualized leadership in order to look at collective leadership and social change. In their study of women leaders from the 1940s to the present, they condemn the descriptive approach to the study of leadership, which has virtually excluded women from most studies of leadership. Thus, they argue that the study of leadership needs to proceed along different dimensions, including the processes, contexts, and outcomes of leadership, and focus on the leader as a catalytic force or facilitator.

The research on minorities, including African Americans, Hispanics, and Asian Americans, is even scantier, although we can expect to see more in the 1990s on cultural differences in style, if any. But for now, the research tends to examine the issues of bias and stereotypes (Bass, 1990). A few studies have examined differences in leadership behaviors between blacks and whites. While some studies of identified leaders did not find differences between blacks and whites, others found that blacks were less willing to support harsh punishments for transgressions of rules (Bass, 1990; Shull and Anthony, 1978).

Studies focusing on the interactive nature of leadership have examined not only the race of the supervisor but also the race of subordinates. Indeed, the perception of leadership, rather than any specific trait, is now the cornerstone of much research in this area. Cross-cultural studies indicate that the nature of the interaction between leader and follower is different across cultures. Thus, there is no universal leadership skill because actions have different meanings within different cultural contexts. The implications of this finding for minorities and for our understanding of the phenomenon of leadership are still unclear. While the research on leadership is voluminous, many questions are still unanswered (Bass, 1990).

Leadership Training

Leadership has been a central concern of adult and continuing educators during the post–World War II era. From the work of Malcolm Knowles to the naming of the practitioner-oriented journal *Adult Leadership,* adult education has often been synonymous with leadership training. Certainly, the work of the Fund for Adult Education and of Sheats, Jayne, and Spence (1953), Essert (1951), and others has focused on the importance of the development of community leadership. In addition, adult educators were pioneers in the area of sensitivity training through the National Training Laboratory in Bethel, Maine. In fact, Schein (1991) suggests that the entire individualistic thrust of today's leadership training can be traced to the National Training Laboratory's emphasis on the individual. He hypothesizes that the "rush to self-actualization" replaced a true concern with leadership.

Following the trends as they emerged, adult and continuing educators adopted the strategies approach to leadership development (Knox, 1982) and are now a part of the current shift to an emphasis on vision and empowerment. Certainly, much of this research on leadership is applicable to adult educators working within institutions and trying to develop new strategies while coping with decreasing resources. But, to give just one example, there seems to be little that these models offer for those seeking to understand the continuing marginality of the field and the concomitant lack of resources from all levels of government. The sole focus on the lack of leadership distracts from a larger, more complex view of the problems.

A central reason for the concern with leadership has been the perceived need to train leaders. This is a recurrent theme throughout the twentieth century. The many revisions of the liberal arts curriculum have often focused on the needs of leaders, but there was little notion in this approach of the necessary skills involved in leadership. The view was that such an education would lead to a well-rounded, informed citizen, whose innate qualities could be nurtured. Certainly, elements of this approach remain in the current writing on vision and transformation (Gardner, 1990).

One of the advantages of the early transactional view of leadership was that it was seen as a skill or set of techniques that could be acquired in a systematic fashion. Building on this view, Knowles and Knowles (1955) wrote about the ways in which adult education methods could be used to encourage leadership development.

Leadership training efforts within organizations are widespread and highly researched, but they focus on the effectiveness and, ultimately, the productivity of those trained. Within these limited purviews, there has been much research into the most efficacious ways of training leaders-managers.

Drawing from the literature of adult development, leadership training in organizations has been conceptualized as a series of stages with a logical progression, starting with needs assessments. Trainers in this area have pioneered different methods, including the top-down and bottom-up approaches to needs assessments. In the former, trainers meet with senior managers in order to determine the kinds of training necessary, whereas the latter approach involves subordinates. Studies have shown that the following content areas are considered the most important in leadership training: feedback to employees, delegation of responsibilities, improvement of listening skills, improvement of personal leadership effectiveness, and encouragement of participation (Bass, 1990).

Research on methods has shown that programs stressing action instead of theory have the greatest result in terms of changed behavior. But while lectures are seen as decidedly unpopular, the research seems to indicate that they can be as effective as discussion groups (Bass, 1990).

Conclusion: Leadership as a Social Problem

In 1950, Alvin Gouldner edited a volume on leadership in which he put forward the view that the recurrent emphasis on leadership needed to be examined more thoroughly. He asked what this concern about leadership indicates about our society and argued that this question needed to be examined in order to understand the reasons for defining leadership in particular ways. For Gouldner, the concern with leadership was conditioned by democratic values and arose out of the belief that leadership was not inherited, either genetically or through status. Only because leadership could be learned could it be viewed as a social problem. "Leadership . . . is as much a social problem as unemployment, housing, or race relations" (Gouldner, 1950, p. 5). Within this frame of reference as a social problem, then, views of leadership are conditioned by specific values.

According to Gouldner, the idea of leadership comes from an increasing sense of alienation in modern society, which values control over the environment. Thus, leaders are people who can accomplish what the alienated and powerless cannot. The most interesting aspect of Gouldner's analysis, however, lies in his view that the preoccupation with leadership is a diversion from "a study of and modification of institutional realities that would impair existent vested interests" (1950, p. 7).

Certainly, Gouldner's concerns have been borne out over the past forty years. Within the United States, leadership research has been preoccupied with examination of the leadership function or interaction within organizations. The notion of transformational leadership introduces the idea of more fundamental change, but, at this point, the model is sketchy and the training of such leaders is not far from the early twentieth-century model of a basic liberal arts education. The central conflict in current writing on leadership involves revitalization and innovation. The issues revolve around two central questions: how to do better what we have always done, or whether we should do something different. Rarely does the writing and research on leadership venture beyond these questions. Only lately, in the writing on women and minorities, have researchers returned to questions about social change as the key aspect of leadership, rather than organizational reform.

The research in leadership has been limited by the narrow definitions applied to it. In particular, we are left studying people who have emerged as "leaders" and then generalizing from their experience. As indicated above, this approach means that because women have not been leaders, they are left out of the analysis and hence seem not to have the requisite leadership attributes derived from the study of men.

Even though the newer paradigms of leaders emphasize vision and the ability to challenge assumptions, they are still limited in their underlying conception of purpose and values. For example, while imagination and innovation are emphasized, even the most humanistic paradigms are still constrained by a model of productivity. Although analysis indicates that the leadership function is to encourage change in existing assumptions, the end is always the same: higher productivity and effectiveness. We need to question more closely the assumption that this model is helpful in developing a vision of adult and continuing education for the twenty-first century.

References

Astin, H. S., and Leland, C. *Women of Influence, Women of Vision: A Cross-Generational Study of Leaders and Social Change.* San Francisco: Jossey-Bass, 1991.

Barnard, C. I. *Organization and Management: Selected Papers.* Cambridge, Mass.: Harvard University Press, 1962.

Bass, B. M. *Bass and Stogdill's Handbook of Leadership Theory, Research, and Managerial Applications.* (3rd ed.) New York: Free Press, 1990.

Bennis, W. G. *Why Leaders Can't Lead: The Unconscious Conspiracy Continues.* San Francisco: Jossey-Bass, 1991.

Bennis, W. G., and Nanus, B. *Leaders: The Strategies for Taking Charge.* New York: HarperCollins, 1985.

Blake, R. R., and Mouton, J. S. *The Managerial Grid.* Houston: Gulf, 1964.

Burns, J. M. *Leadership.* New York: HarperCollins, 1978.

Essert, P. *Creative Leadership of Adult Education.* Englewood Cliffs, N.J.: Prentice Hall, 1951.

Fiedler, F. E. *A Theory of Leadership Effectiveness.* New York: McGraw-Hill, 1967.

Fiedler, F. E. "The Contribution of Cognitive Resources and Behavior to Leadership Performance." In C. F. Graumann and S. Moscovici (eds.), *Changing Conceptions of Leadership.* New York: Springer-Verlag, 1986.

Gardner, J. W. *Excellence: Can We Be Equal and Excellent Too?* New York: HarperCollins, 1961.

Gardner, J. W. *On Leadership.* New York: Free Press, 1990.

Gouldner, A. W. "Introduction." In A. W. Gouldner (ed.), *Studies in Leadership: Leadership and Democratic Action.* New York: HarperCollins, 1950.

Graumann, C. F. "Power and Leadership in Lewinian Field Theory: Recalling an Interrupted Task." In C. F. Graumann and S. Moscovici (eds.), *Changing Conceptions of Leadership.* New York: Springer-Verlag, 1986.

Knowles, M., and Knowles, H. *How to Develop Better Leaders.* New York: Association Press, 1955.

Knox, A. B. (ed.). *Leadership Strategies for Meeting New Challenges,* New Directions for Continuing Education, no. 13. San Francisco: Jossey-Bass, 1982.

Lepsius, M. R. "Charismatic Leadership: Max Weber's Model and Its Applicability to the Rule of Hitler." In C. F. Graumann and S. Moscovici (eds.), *Changing Conceptions of Leadership.* New York: Springer-Verlag, 1986.

Lewin, K. *Field Theory in Social Science.* (D. Cartwright, ed.). New York: HarperCollins, 1951.

McGregor, D. *Leadership and Motivation.* Cambridge, Mass.: MIT Press, 1966.

Morrison, A. M., White, R. P., and Van Velsor, E. *Breaking the Glass Ceiling.* Reading, Mass.: Addison-Wesley, 1987.

Schein, E. H. *Organizational Culture and Leadership: A Dynamic View.* San Francisco: Jossey-Bass, 1991.

Sheats, P. H., Jayne, L. D., and Spence, R. B. *Adult Education: The Community Approach.* New York: Dryden Press, 1953.

Shull, F., and Anthony, W. P. "Do Black and White Supervisory Problem-Solving Styles Differ?" *Personnel Psychology,* 1978, *31,* 761–782.

AMY D. ROSE *is associate professor of adult continuing education at Northern Illinois University, De Kalb.*

*The previous chapters examine dimensions and attributes of
leadership and how those skills can be applied. This chapter addresses
various ways of looking at the future of adult and continuing
education and the challenges for leadership raised by these
speculations.*

Leadership and the Future of Adult and Continuing Education

Paul J. Edelson

In adult and continuing education, leadership's concern with the future is
tied up with trying to provide a sense of stability for the host organization
or the program. By assuming that there is a large measure of continuity
between yesterday, today, and tomorrow, we establish the preconditions
for planning and purposeful action. We want to minimize the uncertainty
that surrounds or envelops human activity—if we "know" the future, we
know what to do and what to avoid. At the same time, we are fully aware
of the precariousness of these projections. Anyone who has worked for
several years within an organization, large or small, can attest to the sudden
changes in direction and policy shifts that take place and the constancy of
change. Being realistic, we are skeptical of our ability to predict the future,
but the alternative of not planning at all is even less attractive.

Attempting to predict the flow of the future in order to provide
direction and to know where and how to deploy organizational resources
make it possible to lead toward a new state rather than just react to altered
circumstances, even if "certainty" is clouded by doubt. The new conditions
may be programming shifts or changes in administrative procedures. Or
the planning activity may result in a changed mission and an entirely new
focus for the adult education unit. The task of maintaining the right balance
between concern for the future and satisfaction of present needs is a prime
leadership responsibility.

The fragility of adult and continuing education—the uncertain funding, the heavy dependence on part-time faculty and staff, the ambiguous
status as an independent and professional field, and the secondary impor-

tance within organizations—contributes, perhaps ironically, to the largely positive attitude that adult and continuing educators have toward the future. It may be that the present beleaguered nature of the field leads us to envision and desire a future with greater stability and prestige. Our optimism may also be owing to our tendency to see adult and continuing education as a force for transformation, change, and progress toward a better world.

Adult educators who attempt to predict the future are influenced by the nature of continuing education, specifically, its ahistorical presentism. By this I mean the acceptance of present context and circumstances as the principal and determining frame of reference. Adult and continuing education is marvelously adaptable to context. It is in some respects a hot-house bloom that becomes remarkably well suited to the environmental conditions of each institution. So much energy is dedicated to honing survival skills such as anticipating imminent organizational changes and doing the job well in the present, albeit at times chaotic, environment that little intellectual capital is devoted to concerns outside of the immediate organization—regional, national, and global developments—that could act as more significant levers of change. One basic recommendation for transcending the present mandates that adult education leaders start opening the information loop and looking or "visioning" beyond our present institutional rabbit holes to fields afar.

Ways of Seeing the Future

Visioning as a technique for seeing the future was popularized by athletes who were encouraged to see within their minds the nuanced performance of their events as a prelude to the actual attempts. Divers, racers, and jumpers rehearsed the minute steps of performance, even trying to feel the wind and water of the stadium and pool.

In a somewhat different vein, visioning has been transplanted to the business sphere with some important modifications. Managers and leaders have been invited to envision the future idealistically, in the sense of describing the type of society that they wish to create through their actions. It is not uncommon for an organizational mission statement to be preceded by a vision statement that projects the organization's mission full-blown onto a changed social landscape that it seeks to bring about. This reification of values and efforts as crystalized actual accomplishment promotes motivation by depicting as attainable that which is merely desired or sought. For example, a continuing education division vision statement may describe a utopian future wherein free adult education is available to all, regardless of means. Like the athlete, we want to believe that if we can think it, we can do it. In this type of visioning, the role of the leader is to help precipitate this vision for and with the staff (Senge, 1990).

But, by what means do we assemble and create these visions of the future and articulate how they are to be obtained? One technique of visioning involves the use of environmental scanning to extrapolate trends from present conditions. Naisbitt (1982) mainstreamed this approach for thousands of readers. Other popular examples in a similar vein include Naisbitt and Aburdene (1990) and Toffler (1971, 1980, 1990).

In looking ahead, we must avoid the notorious pitfall of seeing the future as a linear continuation of the present, thereby predicting variations on an already established theme. For example, prior to the formation of the Organization of Petroleum Exporting Countries (OPEC) cartel, significant leaders in the American automobile industry did not envision the need for impending drastic fuel economy measures. On the other hand, visionary, nonlinear perspectives sometimes seem absurd, only to be later strangely confirmed by events. Science fiction provides the most entertaining examples of these occurrences.

As our current views of the present and short-term futures become more complex, emphasizing nonlinearity and chaos theory, and the uncertain coupling between cause and effect, how much more uncertain do our views become of the comparatively longer-term futures of five and ten years hence? Yet, the need to think ahead as a precondition for action has stimulated the thinking of many in the adult and continuing education field.

Varieties of Adult and Continuing Education Futures

In this section, I review noteworthy examples of visioning in adult education and attempt to identify major thematic areas of concern. Boshier (1981, p. 238), observing the "radical learner centeredness" of the present, predicted that this would be replaced by a future situation where "adult education programming is more geared to the satisfaction of societal and global needs for the attainment and maintenance of biospheric equilibrium." One of his hypothetical scenarios for 1992 predicted that university extension in North America would attract more than 70 percent of university resources!

Long (1983, pp. 181–182) cites the emergence of the electronic cottage and the "availability of powerful electronic media" making for more individualized learning activities. Based on trends and issues identified by Apps (1980), including changing population structures, inflation, consumer movements, the status of women, politics, and mixed attitudes toward education, Long (1983, p. 182) also identified a number of what he called "ambiguous areas" where developmental trends and tendencies were unclear. For example, he noted that while the years of schooling completed by U.S. citizens rose during the period 1969–1981, the ability levels of students declined, with uncertain implications for adult education, including tension between the "second-chance" concept of adult education and the taxpayers' reluctance to support it.

Long also foresaw a greater use of teleconferencing for training as costs of energy and transportation soar, and the centrifugal impact of self-directed learning leading to greater tension and competition between traditional and nontraditional education structures, each with their respective credentials. Product development and marketing would become more important in this highly competitive environment and continuing education bureaus might hire a "special staff of forecasters" (1983, p. 187) to anticipate programming trends. Long's historically and socially based approach prompted him to urge continuing educators to develop a knowledge of adult education history and larger social trends so as to avoid rapid fluctuations in program direction and "abrupt swings in concepts of purpose" (p. 187) that might be prompted by immediate pressures in the local institutional context.

Knowles (1989) also stressed the rapidity and impact of technological change and raised the issue of a "quickening rate of obsolescence of human beings" (p. 131), arguing for a greater emphasis on human functionality tied to an individual's developmental needs, including training. He differentiates between the twentieth- and twenty-first-century requirements for "competent" persons and the nineteenth-century requirements for "knowledgeable" persons. Knowledge by itself is viewed as insufficient to ensure ability in meeting life's challenges.

Knowles (1989, pp. 132–136) projects the need for a Lifelong Learning Research System (LLRS), contrasted with the existing panoply of schools and colleges, as a way of meeting the continuing education needs of adults. LLRS can best be understood as a consortium of institutions of different types and levels. Adults would initially use the services of "educational diagnosticians" and "educational planning consultants" to identify learning activities appropriate to their developmental stages. "Resource people" would subsequently facilitate instructional processes at the appropriate institutional or organizational level.

In these examples of adult education visioning, there is an emerging consensus that the explosive growth of new education technologies will increase choice and enhance opportunities for learner self-directedness. Lewis (1989, p. 620), however, raises the question of whether this brave new world of expanded choice will widen the gap between the literate and the nonliterate poor. And Spear and Mocker (1989, p. 647) also sound a cautionary note, warning that increased informational opportunities through technology and the consequent expanded range of education options may result in "greater [human] diversity and diminished bases for consensus," fractionalizing social community by pushing differentiation among individuals to the limit. This critical perspective evokes a long-standing debate in democratic societies about the proper balance between individual freedoms and attainment, on the one hand, and social responsibility, on the other. Boshier's (1981) utopian projections posit a resolution weighted toward community.

Lewis (1989) and Spear and Mocker (1989) have tried to sensitize adult education leaders to the policy issues embedded in technology. While we encourage its greater use and guide learners to the appropriate learning resources, we need to step back from this taken-for-grantedness of what appear to be technological imperatives and question the implications of our actions. Regardless of our feelings on the resolution of this issue, the need for computer literacy as a basic survival skill becomes even more apparent for adult educators. It is an unavoidable conclusion that we must understand and apply technology in order to evaluate and extend its educational applications.

Fortunately, greater opportunities are available now for developing enhanced competence with electronic, especially computer and telecommunications, media. The virtual ubiquity of computers in most work settings provides opportunities for peer learning in small groups. Many institutions provide free classes to staff members; and even when these classes are not available, the large number of people who are simultaneously coping with aspects of computerization furnishes the requisite critical mass for informal learner networks at the local level. The encouragement and creation of these peer seminars can be a rewarding leadership responsibility. And by moving colleagues collectively into the Information Age in this fashion, we are simultaneously laying the groundwork for future team and cooperative projects.

At the interinstitutional level, it is also possible to interact and learn from colleagues, either directly through electronic mail or through participation in extended electronic networks composed of hundreds, if not thousands, of adult educators around the world. One example is AEDNET, an electronic, computer-mediated adult education network operated by graduate students in the Adult Education Department at Syracuse University. AEDNET offers an information network, runs forums and discussions, and publishes the electronic journal *New Horizons in Adult Education*. *CATALYST* is another continuing education electronic journal, published by the National Council on Community Services, an affiliate of the American Association of Community, Junior, and Technical Colleges.

The seemingly inexorable movement toward greater computerization, coupled with telecommunications and the consequent ease in global communication, has placed a premium on the use of the attendant skills. Reich (1991, pp. 177–178) calls attention to the emergence of a new class of "symbolic analysts" who have become the premier problem solvers of the Information Age. Dealing with abstraction and conceptual issues, symbolic analysts, "solve, identify, and broker problems by manipulating symbols." The higher education levels required to join this elite cohort and the evolving technological base feed the increasing demand for continuing education services.

The consequent redefinition of literacy to include mastery of these new electronic communication skills still further dramatizes the widening gap between advantaged and disadvantaged populations. A higher threshold of educational attainment is necessary for functionality. The same can be said of the escalation of higher education credentials required for occupational attainment. A recent report issued by the American Council on Education (1992) records the quadrupling of the number of master's degrees awarded by American universities from less than 75,000 in 1960 to more than 337,000 in 1991 as this credential has taken on greater significance for career advancement.

In addition to the evolution of technology, adult and continuing educators draw attention to the aging of the U.S. population as a dynamic source of programming opportunities (Merriam and Caffarella, 1991; Fischer, Blazey, and Lipman, 1992). The combination of improved health care for segments of the aging population, still further increasing longevity, and the large number of aging college-educated baby boomers portend much greater opportunities for these groups to continue learning.

Donaldson (1991) strikes out in a different direction from other adult education futurists by looking at possible changes and responses at the institutional level. His images of continuing higher education include the learning network, which is similar to Knowles's LLRS described earlier, and the intellectual front parlor, wherein organizational self-reflection takes place among people from inside and outside of the organization. Donaldson advocates a "missionary vision" and zeal by adult education leaders if they wish to be successful in realizing these two images of adult learning.

Implications for Leadership

What should the response of adult and continuing education leadership be to these speculations and projections? Do they provide road maps to the future with specific destinations, landmarks, and instructions? Or do they instead function as compasses that offer just general directions?

Ideally, our knowledge, or speculation, about the future will be of help in optimizing choices for both the short and long runs. If this is in fact our premise, should we then work deductively and fashion programming decisions based on developments that we believe are taking place? And even if we, as leaders, could with confidence follow this course of action, do we then simply manufacture a future that we believe is appropriate and then transmit this to others on our staffs for purposes of implementation?

This line of thought, based on a notion of the leader as the great problem solver for the organization, is inconsistent with what some people now think about the limits of leadership. They question the superior

wisdom and prescience of leaders and instead stress empowering dimensions that encourage other members of the organization to develop their
own problem-solving skills. Following this line of reasoning, it may be less
important for the leader to develop a plausible view of the future—either
road map or compass—than it is for multiple perspectives to emerge from
among staff members.

In effect, leaders can use studying and thinking about the future as a
device for promoting continuing education by staff members. By encouraging everyone to become a futurist, leaders can stimulate all members of
the organization to think about the larger environments within which
continuing education plays a role.

Becoming Futurists

We require a way of thinking about the future that renders us self-
conscious of its predictive limitations. Our goal is to deepen our understanding of the present by examining aspects of contemporary society,
even if we are unable to predict their precise developmental directions. In
this modified approach to linear futurism, we do not assume continuity
from a single fixed point outward. Instead, we encourage scenario building
based on multiple extrapolations and interpretations of the present for
several futures.

The visioning technique of scenario building is recommended by
Schwartz (1991). He describes how the Royal Dutch/Shell Oil Company
successfully employed this approach during the early 1970s in thinking
about international oil supplies prior to the 1973 OPEC embargo. By
conceptualizing the then unthinkable—Middle Eastern Islamic oil-pro-
ducing countries acting in concert against the economically developed and
oil-dependent West—Shell was in a position to capitalize on OPEC's
tightening of supply and the resulting energy crisis. Shell was emotionally
prepared for the change and, in a scenario developed for a fictionalized oil
crisis, had anticipated the development of other oil sources in non-Islamic
countries and in the North Sea. Shell rose from among the weaker oil-
producing companies to become one of the two largest.

Schwartz views scenario building as more than the spreading of bets
over several possible futures. Instead, he sees it as a way of inculcating a
flexibility toward alternative developments, promoting a confidence toward unforeseen occurrences, whatever they may be, and extending cre-
ativity about a range of alternative actions. Schwartz considers scenario
building as a way of learning. The result is not a more accurate picture of
tomorrow but better decision making when the future becomes the present.

Using an approach of multiple scenario visioning for adult education,
we could start by raising a basic question: Which activities, programs, and
courses should the continuing education unit emphasize in the next five

years?" Typically, we never face a question like this in a premeditated, coordinated way but instead back into the future on the basis of very small incremental steps whose cumulative final outcomes we never fully appreciate initially. We end up in the future! For example, beliefs in the continuity of state funding for continuing education credit programs and in the persistence of favorable economic trends could, over time, cause a continuing education unit to be highly dependent on this single source of revenue, which suddenly is jeopardized by a recession. The hypothetical continuing education unit is suddenly threatened with a loss of state funding (which is based on sales tax revenue) that lessens its ability to meet learner needs.

Through a multiple scenario approach, an attempt is made to anticipate how current trends and developments can make for a contested or uncertain future. The approach followed by Schwartz involves the creation of several teams to develop separate scenarios for the future. The teams can bring together those who are not customarily associated in the work flow, thereby promoting mutual understanding and teamwork. By affording the opportunity for individuals to consider the larger adult education program from wider and different perspectives, the teams encourage holistic thinking about the entire organization, not just the parts.

A possible methodology for adult and continuing education visioning teams is to develop scenarios based on how they see the world, nation, and region developing. The important task for each group is to ask questions that generate thinking and then to develop "plots" for how the future may actually evolve. For example, an adult and continuing education division engaged in visioning developed alternative scenarios based on either a worsening or improving of the state economy. In the scenario of the worsening economy, there was continuing financial pressure on the state's education institutions, causing them to emphasize both traditional core activities and programs that can generate increased funds or else increase the possibility of generating more funds. Under the conditions of this scenario, continuing education was pressed, like the host organization, to become more self-sustaining. But the scenario, as it developed, also suggested several possible approaches to this predicament.

By addressing the needs of the unemployed in a more deliberate fashion, the continuing education unit could make itself eligible for new state funding established for this group. Beyond generating funds, the unit's positive impact in meeting regional needs would also be a source of excellent public relations for the university, which in the past was considered too aloof from the local community.

In addressing the needs of the unemployed, the continuing education unit would also have to develop among its staff enhanced counseling and career development skills. These staff skills could also be marketed to businesses concerned about downsizing their labor pools and to individuals who, though not unemployed, are concerned about the future labor market and how it could develop. The adult and continuing education division in the worsening economy scenario thus reoriented itself to career development as a major theme.

A second scenario, built around the plot of an improving economy, was rosier than the first scenario. It entailed gradual restoration of full funding for school districts, colleges, and universities and an eventual return to business as usual. Both credit and noncredit continuing education activities were buoyed by expanding economic growth, domestic and international, and by optimism. The expansion of business stimulated people to develop their skills in response to opportunities in the evolving job market and in response to their own preferences.

In these visioning sessions, both teams highlighted the need for quality career development services as a key to integrating continuing education activity. Appreciating the value of career development as an organizing concept that is viable in both types of economic climates, the entire school began repositioning itself and its activities—credit and noncredit—around this role, which was complementary with the theme of lifelong learning that had permeated the division's literature.

By working together on the scenario teams, all members of the staff were involved in confronting the future and in developing possible responses. They were now prepared to interpret career development in each aspect of their work, rather than to follow an ambiguous directive from the dean's office. This adult and continuing education unit's response to the future—helping people to cope with innovation and uncertainty, and interpreting and making sense of change—is consistent with other, well-established continuing education missions.

The scenario-building exercise could produce different outcomes if tried again at a later point. But the plots are less important than success in having staff members work together as teams to anticipate future developments before a crisis forces a sudden choice on the unit. An even less pleasant circumstance would consist of being handed a fait accompli from the university administration without even having the opportunity to consider alternatives.

Implicit in scenario building is the lack of stability and security in committing to one future as opposed to another. We need to develop sufficient mental agility to take advantage of the unpredictable randomness of change. At the very least, as an outcome of visioning, we must develop flexible ways of dealing with the present as it unfolds. Ironically, the malleability and amorphousness of adult and continuing education (Edelson, 1991) can be its greatest asset.

As pointed out earlier, institutions become powerful filters of information and influences on behavior. Leaders must learn to experiment beyond what institutions "want" of adult and continuing education and try to seek out opportunities that are challenging and enlarging. Visioning can be seen as part of a twofold agenda that satisfies existing official institutional priorities and, at the same time, creates new scenarios for adult education that are more flexible and profession-driven.

Tomorrow's adult and continuing education leaders are at the cutting edge of the present. They are better informed about people and organizations. They can employ multiple perspectives for looking at problems and, as learners, can function as parts of teams, not necessarily always as captains. They draw on the expanding knowledge base of adult education and a wider variety of literature to generate fresh, even unconventional ideas. The new leaders can relate their intimate knowledge of institutional context to historical and social trends. Effective communication skills in both traditional and electronic media facilitate participation with colleagues all over the globe. Overall, tomorrow's leaders are actively engaged in improving adult and continuing education and in making a better world.

References

American Council on Education. "A Profile of Master's Degree Recipients and Students." *Higher Education and National Affairs,* Apr. 20, 1992, p. 3.

Apps, J. W. "Six Influences on Adult Education in the 1980's." *Lifelong Learning: The Adult Years,* 1980, 3 (10), 4–7.

Boshier, R. W. "Adult Education: Issues of the Future." In B. W. Kreitlow and Associates, *Examining Controversies in Adult Education.* San Francisco: Jossey-Bass, 1981.

Donaldson, J. F. "New Opportunities or a New Marginality: Strategic Issues in Continuing Higher Education." *Continuing Higher Education Review,* 1991, 55 (3), 120–128.

Edelson, P. J. "Model Building and Strategic Planning in Continuing Higher Education." *New Horizons in Adult Education,* 1991, 5 (2), 15–25.

Fischer, R. B., Blazey, M. L., and Lipman, H. T. *Students in the Third Age: University/College Programs for Retired Adults.* New York: Macmillan, 1992.

Knowles, M. S. *The Making of an Adult Educator: An Autobiographical Journey.* San Francisco: Jossey-Bass, 1989.

Lewis, L. H. "New Educational Technologies for the Future." In S. B. Merriam and P. M. Cunningham (eds.), *Handbook of Adult and Continuing Education.* San Francisco: Jossey-Bass, 1989.

Long, H. B. *Adult and Continuing Education: Responding to Change.* New York: Teachers College Press, 1983.

Merriam, S. B., and Caffarella, R. S. *Learning in Adulthood: A Comprehensive Guide.* San Francisco: Jossey-Bass, 1991.

Naisbitt, J. *Megatrends: Ten New Directions Transforming Our Lives.* New York: Warner Books, 1982.

Naisbitt, J., and Aburdene, P. *Megatrends 2000: Ten New Directions for the 1990s.* New York: William and Morrow, 1990.

Reich, R. E. *The Work of Nations: Preparing Ourselves for 21st Century Capitalism.* New York: Knopf, 1991.

Schwartz, P. *The Art of the Long View: Planning for the Future in an Uncertain World.* New York: Doubleday/Currency, 1991.

Senge, P. *The Fifth Discipline: The Art and Practice of the Learning Organization.* New York: Doubleday/Currency, 1990.

Spear, G. E., and Mocker, D. W. "The Future of Adult Education." In S. B. Merriam and P. M. Cunningham (eds.), *Handbook of Adult and Continuing Education*. San Francisco: Jossey-Bass, 1989.

Toffler, A. *Future Shock*. New York: Random House, 1971.

Toffler, A. *The Third Wave*. New York: William and Morrow, 1980.

Toffler, A. *Power Shift: Knowledge, Wealth, and Violence at the Edge of the 21st Century*. New York: Bantam, 1990.

PAUL J. EDELSON is dean of the School of Continuing Education and director of the Continuing Education Research Center at the State University of New York, Stony Brook.

INDEX

ORDERING INFORMATION

NEW DIRECTIONS FOR ADULT AND CONTINUING EDUCATION is a series of paperback books that explores issues of common interest to instructors, administrators, counselors, and policy makers in a broad range of adult and continuing education settings—such as colleges and universities, extension programs, businesses, the military, prisons, libraries, and museums. Books in the series are published quarterly in spring, summer, fall, and winter and are available for purchase by subscription as well as by single copy.

SUBSCRIPTIONS for 1992 cost $45.00 for individuals (a savings of 20 percent over single-copy prices) and $60.00 for institutions, agencies, and libraries. Please do not send institutional checks for personal subscriptions. Standing orders are accepted.

SINGLE COPIES cost $14.95 when payment accompanies order. (California, New Jersey, New York, and Washington, D.C., residents please include appropriate sales tax.) Billed orders will be charged postage and handling.

DISCOUNTS FOR QUANTITY ORDERS are available. Please write to the address below for information.

ALL ORDERS must include either the name of an individual or an official purchase order number. Please submit your order as follows:
    Subscriptions: specify series and year subscription is to begin
    Single copies: include individual title code (such as CE1)

MAIL ALL ORDERS TO:
    Jossey-Bass Publishers
    350 Sansome Street
    San Francisco, California 94104

FOR SALES OUTSIDE OF THE UNITED STATES CONTACT:
    Maxwell Macmillan International Publishing Group
    866 Third Avenue
    New York, New York 10022